FAST TRACK TO COMMISSIONS

Success TV, LLC

Cover Design: Steve Miljat
Interior Design: Tressa Foster
Production Management: Success TV, LLC

Dedication

I can't just mention a few names of friends and relatives as a dedication of this book because reaching this point in my life and business is really all about these people. Their place in my life is the reason this book is in print.

My Dad—You are my hero. I strive every day to become the man you are. I can't thank you enough for the support and unconditional love you have given me throughout life. You have taught me how to be a successful entrepreneur and build an ethical long-term business model. You have been key to the majority of my success. But, the most important thing you ever taught me while growing up was the importance to be a man of good character. Before I make any decisions, be them personal or business, I always think of a sentence you said to me when I was around 12 years old - "Your character is defined by the decisions you make when no one else is looking". That one sentence is solely responsible for every choice I have ever made since then, and will continue to make for the rest of my life.
I hope one day when people speak of me they reference the exact same qualities they attribute to you today. Thank you for all of the love, support and guidance you have given me, you're an amazing father and I love you so much.

My Mom—To my mother, you're the backbone of the family. You're the most caring person I know in this world. You've always had my back and shown me what a strong person is and how to become one. Thank you so much for supporting all of my decisions and teaching me how to be independent. You raised me to be a loving person and realize the importance of helping others, no matter my current situation. I wouldn't be who I am today, nor would I have the success I have, without your consistent influence on my everyday decisions in both life and business. I love you so much.

My Brother Anthony— Watching you grow into a successful entrepreneur while I was a kid was key to my success. You took me under your wing and taught me how to be a successful businessman and what it means to be a good person and give back to others when you achieve success. You've shown me that success is worthless unless you're able to share it with the ones you love. I've always admired your whole heart and ability to stay ethical and not get pulled into bad decisions. If it weren't for you I wouldn't be where I am today, end of story. You are the true image of a man with good character and have been a role model of mine since we were just kids selling boxes of chocolate from door to door to buy dad that bike for Christmas. Thank you for everything and I love you.

continued on next page

My Sister Brittian—Thanks for always being there for me. You're just like Mom in your strength, intelligence and dedication to the ones you love. Your passion for doing things you love is admirable and rare. I'm so lucky to have you and love you very much.

My Grandmother, Nanny—You are the sweetest and funniest grandmother one could ask for. Thank you for always making it a point to call me throughout the weeks during my travels and remind me that you're thinking of me and love me. I love re-listening to your voicemails from time to time when I need cheering up! You are amazing, and thank you for bringing so much light into my life!

Kaci—10 years ago when I met you and had absolutely nothing, you showed me unconditional love. You took care of me. You worked waiting tables overnight so I didn't have to have a job and could study for all of my college classes. You've been right by my side through thick and thin. You've been a key factor in all of the success I enjoy. You've always been bright in giving me ideas online that have created tons of success for me. You've been so great to sit right by my side every night while I was building this business, not going out with friends, but staying in with me and supporting me.
You've completed me for the past decade and will continue to do so throughout the rest of my life, I love you.

Uncle Lynn and Aunt Julie—Thank you for all of your support and love. The support you've given me throughout my life is priceless and I'm so lucky to have ya'll.

My Best Friend LB—You are no less than a brother to me. It's been amazing to watch you grow from one of my first students to an independently successful businessman online. Seeing your success is part of what opened my eyes to how great it feels to teach others and help them to reach their goals in life. For that, I thank you. Continue doing what you are doing and always strive to do better. Love you bro.

Josh—Thank you for all of your support and guidance. I look to you as another big brother. You've always been there for me, had my back, and played a large role in teaching me what it means to make good business decisions and to be selfless. Also, thanks for helping me put the basketball goal up in my backyard! I love you man.

RB—You've been a valuable business partner and friend. Thank you for the guidance and friendship over the past years. I credit a lot of my success to a few conversations we had. I wish you the best and continued success.

Contents

Introduction

Welcome to the first page of a life-changing experience. I'm Adrian Morrison, and I became a millionaire at the age of 24. I didn't inherit money. I didn't work 80 hours a week. I didn't start a business with inventory, employees, and a building. And I didn't break any laws.

What I do to earn pots full of money is spend a few enjoyable hours each day on my computer, and much of that time is just checking how much money came into my account since yesterday and tracking my marketing campaigns. I use the concept of leverage to the hilt to generate affiliate marketing commissions from the Internet.

I leverage my time, my websites and blogs, and my social network memberships to present thousands of products to millions of consumers every day on the Web. It's called affiliate marketing because I'm an affiliate for many other companies and businesses, and they pay me to bring them customers.

I have to dial back for a minute now, as you may be getting a reading on your "hype-meter." That's because it sounds so easy, and we've all been taught that the road to riches isn't easy, and nothing easy ever amounts to much. So let me approach it from a different perspective.

At the beginning of your affiliate marketing business, you'll spend time setting up your marketing sites, blogs, and social media accounts. You'll spend time setting up affiliate accounts with companies and advertisers who will be paying you those commissions. So, from a time perspective, it's not easy to get going.

And you never stop testing and evaluating your marketing in order to improve your profits, so time will always be a requirement for the riches you can enjoy. What isn't required is a large investment of money. In fact, you'll never have to spend a dime if you don't want to.

So let's get right down to what I'm going to provide for you in this book that will make you totally confident in the knowledge that you can do what I did. You can be a millionaire without a building, employees, or any significant investment of money.

Some of the marketing tools you'll learn to use may be things you're involved in already. If you're a Facebook, Twitter, or Google+ user, you're already working with tools that can be turned into commission profits from home.

If you already work with a website or blog, you have the basic tools and knowledge to jumpstart your affiliate marketing business and begin to see cash flowing into your bank account via the Internet.

This isn't a book full of encouraging platitudes or "you can do it" statements. It is a book that gives you hard knowledge and specific detailed instructions on how to use the Internet to bring customers to businesses that will gladly pay you each and every time a customer buys a product when they arrive from your marketing efforts. You'll be encouraged and confident simply because you know that what you've learned works and that you can replicate my success.

- Each marketing medium is examined for its income-producing potential.
- Specific techniques and marketing strategies are delivered to you for each marketing media.
- Third party tools are delivered that multiply your efforts and leverage your time to spread your marketing over multiple sites and social media venues.
- Common sense affiliate marketing business strategies are explained in order to assure your success without waste of time or money.

Thanks for reading this introduction; it's simply a highly condensed overview of a comprehensive affiliate marketing business plan and structure. That plan and structure will make you rich … if you just keep reading.

CHAPTER 1
Commissions from Where & How?

This chapter title is a fair question to ask before you take off
and read the rest of this book. I don't want you reading future chapters trying to discover if this book can really change
your financial future. I want you to be so excited from what
you read in this first chapter that you won't be able to put the
book down. You'll want to keep reading, as each chapter is just
building your business plan, while this one tells you what that
plan is.

I could have titled this book *Money from Mouse to Wallet,*
since that's a simple statement of what you're going to learn in
these pages. I'm going to give you operating instructions for a
business you can operate from home with unlimited potential,
low-to-no overhead, and the flexibility to let you run it from
the beach, ski resort, or a hunting cabin if you want. First, let's
talk about what it's not. What comes to mind for many people
when I mention commission income is not what you're going to
get from this book.

The Kind of Business This Isn't

Don't start looking for investors or a bank to rob to finance a large building in a retail area of town. Don't start adding up potential operating costs, like utilities, employee salaries, insurance, and other brick and mortar store costs. This isn't going to require a building, purchased or rented, at all.

What about inventory? You can't sell something if you don't have it in stock in the retail environment … at least not in the brick and mortar type business. Well, forget about inventory, too. You don't need it. Of course, when there's no inventory, the costs of maintaining it, like theft loss and storage, go away as well.

OK, But Commissions Require Work

Forget punching a time clock, and don't even think about knocking on doors or scheduling sales appointments. Sure, that's how millions of sales people earn commissions every day. However, we're going to earn our commissions without those activities, and without limiting our income to our individual time available for direct selling.

Think of yourself as a cloned super-salesperson. You're able to create as many of you as you need in order to one-on-one with millions ... no tens of millions of people. You don't have to watch a clock, since your clones don't sleep or eat, and they work 24/7/365.

I'm not even going to agree with the statement that "commissions require work," at least not in the sense you're probably thinking about "work." I'm going to teach you everything you need to know in this book about putting commission income into your bank account through planning, business structure, and management, not through hourly or direct sales work.

Now you might still think of that as work. But let me tell you what's FUN in my everyday life. It's waking up every morning, turning on my computer, and checking my income reports for the amount of money I made last night ... while I was sleeping. Or it's spending the day skiing, and checking my computer before going out for dinner to see how my much fatter my account is since my first trip up the lift.

We're going to use something that stock market investors use every day to try and make money: leverage. They borrow against existing assets to buy more, leveraging their financial ability to make money. That's making money if they don't lose in a risky market.

We're going to leverage your desire and the knowledge and tools you'll get from this book to take your profits to the bank. It's not going to be in the slightest bit risky, either. We're going to leverage what you learn here to build a business that can grow as large as you desire with no employees and no 60 hour work weeks.

OK, now that you know what it's not, let's see the big picture about what this business is.

Commissions the Affiliate Marketing Way

In the next chapter I'll give you a thorough overview, with examples, of how affiliate marketing works with many varied products and services. For now, let's take a step back to look at the big picture of how I'm going to guarantee your ability to rake in commission income through our leveraging process.

It's All Done Online

First, you don't need any more of a business presence than a laptop computer. If you don't have a computer, use one for free at the library or on-the-cheap at a local Internet café. This business requires no inventory or location, other than online locations. I'll show you how to create these at little or no cost, your choice.

Your computer literally becomes a cash machine, only you don't have to deposit the cash before you withdraw it. You take what I'm going to provide for you here in the way of information, tools, and resources, and you build an Internet cash machine that doesn't require your close supervision. It just spits out cash 24/7/365.

Companies Pay You Commissions to Be Their Marketer on the Web

The basic concept is simple; you go on the Internet and advertise products and services on behalf of companies, and they pay you a commission when you get them a sale or deliver a customer. This commission can be a percentage of a sale amount, or it can be a flat dollar amount. And if the product or service is some type of ongoing subscription with future payments, you may even get commissions on those future payments, as well.

Why don't they just do it themselves, especially large well-funded corporations? Actually they are engaged in large budget Internet advertising. So what do they need you for? Take a huge consumer products company, or maybe a chain electronics store like Best Buy. They have an enormous website, and a full staff to maintain it and to process orders. So again, why do they need us?

That enormous website is still just one website of hundreds of millions out there on the Internet. And tens of thousands of those sites are electronics retailers. True, Best Buy has a brand name presence and recognition, but that doesn't mean that every Web buyer looking for a cell phone battery will end up on their site.

There's even a drawback in marketing from a gigantic website with several hundred thousand products across a broad spectrum of electronics, appliance, music, and software categories. It's mind-boggling what you can buy there, and it's no quick trick to get to that particular cell phone battery or DVD player that's just right for you.

People Buy on Impulse, Information & Recommendation

Those three things don't go together all of the time. People may buy on impulse when the timing and the offer is right. However, people definitely buy on information. What does that mean? People find the Internet of great value in research-ing products and services, learning more about them, and even in reading reviews or comments by their social media contacts and friends. And people buy when they receive trusted word of mouth referrals from their friends and online contacts.

It's true that all of the information they need to know about a certain DVD player's features and specifications is right there with the item at the Best Buy website. However, how does a customer come to be seeing that particular item's details on their screen when they're in the buying mode?

- Their destination was the Best Buy site and they searched and researched the many DVD players there to get to the one they decided to buy.
- They saw an online display advertisement for this specific DVD player on a movie rental site.
- They were reading a blog that reviews items like this and found this one specifically with good review comments about the features they wanted the most.
- They were online at Facebook, Twitter, Google+, MySpace, or LinkedIn, and someone they know was talking about this model.
- Same places but the general discussion was about DVD players and there was a display ad for this one.

There could be other ways they ended up at this item on Best Buy, but these are the most common. Now how many of those were likely to be ads placed by the manufacturer or Best Buy? Sure, they all could have been, but I'm here to tell you that all but the first bullet could have been, and likely were, the activities of an affiliate marketer.

Affiliates Get Commissions for Results

What do I mean by getting commissions for results? Isn't it only logical that you won't get paid unless someone buys something? Actually, a lot of affiliates make a lot of money when absolutely no credit card transaction takes place! Let's expand the meaning of the term "results."

An advertiser or consumer products company may have a number of reasons for not going for a sale in their first customer interaction. It could be that their product is a higher-end item that requires a bit more selling than can usually be done on a web page. Or they may have found that their conversion rate (turning prospects into customers) is much higher if they offer a free trial for a subscription product or service.

Netflix is a great example. This company has paid a huge number of affiliates a monstrous amount of money for tens of millions of small commission transactions that resulted only in a free trial subscription. Netflix knew that they would keep the vast majority of those trial members, converting them to paid memberships, so the company would pay a few dollars each to any affiliate who sent them to the free trial offer.

For higher-end items, such as high dollar furnishings, clothing, or even fitness and exercise DVD series, companies might pay the affiliate to deliver a prospect who takes the desired action. That action might be ordering a free trial, or it might be giving their email address for something in return, then the company markets them with email.

So, while the vast majority of affiliate commissions are paid for the actual purchase of a product or service, there are loads of opportunities to get paid even if no money changes hands when you deliver the prospect.

The Delivery and Payment Logistics

The Internet and technology has changed our lives for the better in most cases. When it comes to what may appear to be the complex process of tracking people's movements on the Internet and how they came to be at a certain page, it's not as complex as you might think.

The Affiliate Link or Image/Banner Ad

The most common way for advertisers (who you work for) to track publishers (us) and their referrals of prospects and customers is through the use of Banner/Image Ads and affiliate links. Even the ads will have a link, since it's the way you are identified so that you can be paid.

So you're out there placing these ads or links, and we'll go into great detail about how and where you place them, and you want your advertiser customer to know it was you who delivered the customer so that you get paid.

This is an example of a vertical banner ad that the advertiser provides to their affiliates to use in their marketing.

The ad in this case is a food special at a restaurant, or it could be for a supermarket deal. The ad itself is designed by professionals for your use as a publisher, and that's great for you.

You don't pay for this high dollar creative and marketing expertise. You get to use it for free … and get paid!

The ad itself doesn't get you paid; it just gets the prospect's attention. The link associated with the ad is how the prospect is tracked and the publisher is paid. It will have a code in it that identifies the publisher in the advertiser's affiliate system for payment if the prospect takes the desired action.

https://members.cj.com/member/ publisher/other/getlinkdetail.do?a dId=10908673&crumbTrail=13280 210xxxxx

This is an example of an affiliate link, and actually one for that ad above. One of the two numbers in the link identifies the publisher, so they get paid when they should. Many times you are not using a display ad, image, or banner. You are often just using the link as a "text link." How does that work with that really looooooong link?

Text links are those that are used with specific text, and the long link itself isn't visible. Let's look at an example of how this might be used with this link:

I'm saving tons of money with my <u>fast food deal of the day</u>! The underlined text is what the site visitor or reader sees and clicks on as a link. The long link text and numbers is where they actually go from that text link.

Now you can see that, as a publisher, you can be all over the Internet placing hundreds or thousands of these links to all sorts of products and services. In most cases you don't pay a dime to place them, though we'll talk later about paid advertising and how to make it a no-risk profit generator.

Baked Cookies are Good – Web Cookies are Better!

They're called cookies, but they don't come from the oven. Many sites that you visit place what is called a cookie on your computer's hard drive. That's how the website remembers who you are, or your special settings, or the places you like to visit on the site. For the most part, cookies are useful, and we want them for many sites we visit.

In affiliate marketing, cookies can mean repeat income, or de-layed income. When a prospect clicks on an affiliate link, many advertisers will place a timed cookie on that prospect's hard drive. By timed, I mean that there is an expiration date for how long the cookie stays there.

This cookie placement allows a number of things that are great for affiliate marketers. First, you don't need to link to a specific product or promotion on a site. Let's say that you're affiliate marketing for a large electronics website, and you send prospects there without a clear idea of what they will end up buying.

The cookie that's placed will make sure that you are the affiliate who gets credit for the sale and the commission, no matter where they end up on the site. And that includes if they buy multiple items on that visit.

Better than that, many times the timed cookie will also get you paid again if that customer returns and buys something else while the cookie is still active. So if your advertiser places a 90 day cookie when you send the prospect, they may buy something during that visit or they may not. However, if they return one or more times before that cookie expires, you get paid.

Now You Know – It's Time to Explore the Possibilities!
That's the broad overview of how affiliate marketing and commissions work. The potential for income is greater than you can even imagine right now, but I'm going to show you more to help you get your commissions from your home business set up and bringing in cash.

CHAPTER 2

Affiliate Marketing Basics

In the previous chapter, we covered the big picture basics of affiliate marketing and how you get paid as a publisher. What I want to do now is to make sure you know some technology basics about how you're going to place these banner ads and links around the Internet.

Actually, the image gets the point across, as we're "linking for dollars." From the first chapter, you know why you want to place ads and links, but let's make sure that those of us who are possibly technologically challenged understand the basics of placing them around the Web.

Placing Text Links

You learned in the previous chapter that text links can be a very long and complicated affiliate link that's the destination when a simple bit of text is clicked on. One method is allowing the advertiser to provide you with the link HTML. Here are some of the banner and text ad choices offered by BedandBreakfast.com.

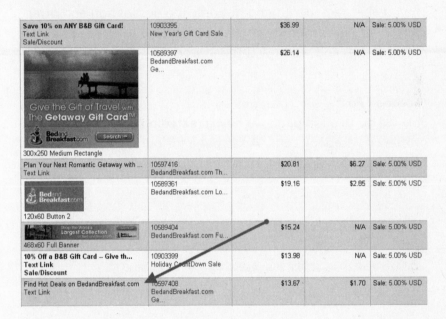

The one at the arrow is for a text link, so let's look at the HTML that this advertiser provides when we ask for that link code:

<a href="http://www.kqzyfj.com/click-5296213-10597408" target="_top">Find Hot Deals on BedandBreakfast.com</a><img src="http://www.awltovhc.com/image-5296213-10597408" width="1" height="1" border="0"/>

However, here's what it looks like when embedded into a website:
<u>Find Hot Deals on BedandBreakfast.com</u>

You're going to be doing a lot of writing about products and services on websites, blogs, and in social media. In these cases, you can just grab the destination URL and link your desired text to it. In the example above, this is the actual destination URL:

http://www.kqzyfj.com/click-5296213-10xxxx08

The numbers are identifying not only the destination and offer, but the affiliate's identity, as well. So let's go to some social network sites and see how this will work:

Facebook Post
First we go to a fan page we have created on our personal profile on Facebook.com. A fan page for our sales niche is better, but not important in this example. We want to post an update, so:

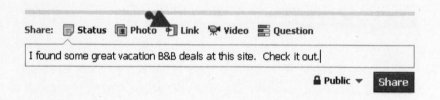

I typed in some text about finding great deals at this site, and then click on the "Link" button.

I paste in the link, and click on the Attach button, for this:

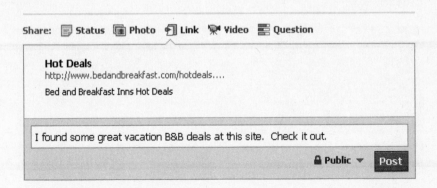

You can see that Facebook placed the link for me, even picking up text from the destination page. Now all I have to do is to click on the Post button, and I'm in business!

Twitter
Twitter limits your post to a set number of characters, so long links aren't a good thing. However, Twitter shortens those for you. So when you're typing in your Tweet text, paste in the long link and Twitter will shorten it for you. You can also use your own desired link-shortening service, which is useful not only in Twitter but in many sites where you'll be posting. Let's look at one:

Link Shortening Service
There are several online services to convert long links to short ones. One of these is http://bit.ly, and here is how it works:

You paste in your long affiliate link and simply click the Shorten button.

The service shortens the link, and you use this shortened version in your sites, blogs, and posts.

LinkedIn Post

Particularly for marketing products and services of interest to business owners and managers, you'll be writing posts and answering questions at LinkedIn.com.

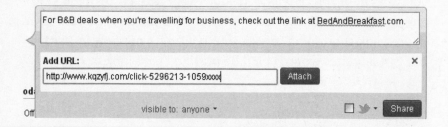

It's much the same as Facebook, with your text about the link, and the text can be much longer, educational, informational, etc. Then you attach the link and share the post.

Google+

At the time I'm writing this, Google+ is coming on strong as a major social media site. It's going to be a great marketing site as well, allowing business pages for our affiliate marketing purposes.

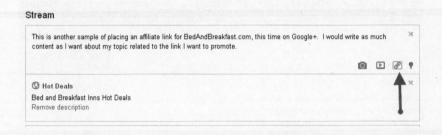

I simply write as much text as I want, and just like Facebook and LinkedIn, I paste my link into a small window that comes up when I click on the small link chain icon. Google+ grabs the website destination page text and places it, including an image in some cases.

Affiliate Banner Ads

Banner ads are another way to advertise your affiliate links. Many affiliate marketers use them on their own websites or blogs.

The B&B example can be used again here. The image above shows one of their banner ads for affiliate marketer use. You can see that the HTML code is provided, and you can drop it right into your website or blog with a copy/paste.

The image above shows the creation of a blog post or web page using WordPress software. By typing my text and then pasting in the banner HTML that I copied from the advertiser, I get this:

The post or page is placed on the site with the banner ad, and I make money if my visitor clicks and takes the desired action at the site.

Another approach is to pay to place your banner ads on sites that have highly relevant content. In this case, Travel Sites would be a great place to put the ad. Generally, these are placed with payment by CPM, payment based on how many thousand times the ad is seen, or "impressions."

Post About B&B Travel Deals

Posted by ██████ • January 31, 2012 • 🖨 Printer-friendly

👍 Like   📘 Be the first of your friends to like this.

+1 This is an example of a WordPress blog post to promote an affiliate link for BedAndBreakfast.com. I can have a more square shaped banner ad in the sidebar of my site or blog, or I can put it right into the post, like this:

The image is one of many sites that sell banner advertising spots to affiliate marketers and advertisers. Note that there is a banner ad running for an airport shuttle service at the top of this page that is an example of their advertising opportunities.

I wanted you to know about paid marketing, but you don't need to spend money to get started and become highly profitable in the affiliate marketing business. You can also pay for search engine marketing, SEM, with Google Adwords and Yahoo Search Marketing. I'll give you the details in a chapter about SEM later.

It's About Relevance

You're up on the basics of placing affiliate text links, as well as banner and image ads. However, there's a really important concept to keep in mind for profitability and efficiency. The concept is relevance. It's not just *what* links and ads you're placing, it's *where* you place them.

I touched on this with the paid banner ads for B&B reservations being placed on travel sites. It's the logical place to have an ad for places to stay when travelling, so it could be a wise decision, even if you're paying for the placement.

However, relevance is critical in free placement as well, and that's what you'll be doing the most and probably exclusively at the beginning. You don't have to pay for ad placement to make money in affiliate marketing. In fact, I'm saying that you shouldn't think about it when you start out. I'm going to show you how to make a ton of money for free.

Here are the locations and site types where you'll be placing affiliate links and possibly banners and image ads:
• your own websites, possibly very focused mini-sites
• your own blogs that are individually niche-oriented
• social media
  - Facebook fan pages
  - Google+ business pages
  - LinkedIn
  - Twitter
  - MySpace
• article sites
• comments on individual and company websites and blogs

These are all going to be really profitable places for your marketing. However, they'll only be profitable if you keep with the "relevance" mantra. Don't run diet supplement ads on an electronics website, or vice versa.

For those diet supplements, build your own fitness-oriented website or blog, comment on those types of websites and blogs, and place them in diet and fitness discussions and pages in the social media.

Now you have the basics. Place your advertising on sites and in discussions that are relevant to the type or market niche. The visitors to those sites will have an interest in your topic, since they're already reviewing that type of information or engaging in discussions relevant to your niche.

Advertise, Track Results & Modify

Lastly, when it comes to basics, you're never finished adapting your strategies, links, banners, and placement. Your affiliate links, whether from a network or individual advertisers, will provide good tracking, as you'll be able to access reports with your income by advertiser and by link or banner ad.

For this reason, you may want to try not to duplicate use of the very same link or banner ad on multiple sites, as you may not be able to tell where the click originated. Use varied links and ads for different sites, even if for the same product or advertiser destination site.

When we get to the information about affiliate networks, we'll see more about the tracking of performance for a publisher's advertising both by advertiser client and by specific link. As you build out your business, you'll use these reports to drop some advertisers, change links and ads, and move them to different sites or blogs.

Those are the basics. Before we get into specifics and detailed guides for making your business happen, let's raise your excitement level a bit by showing you how you can market just about anything you want, even sticking only to those market niches in which you have a personal interest.

CHAPTER 3

If It Sells, It Sells Through Affiliates

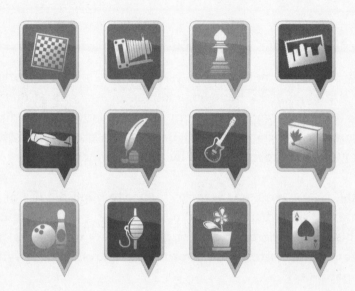

What's better than spending almost nothing, being off more than you're working, and watching your bank account mushroom with affiliate marketing? The trick is to sell stuff that is of great interest to you. I talk to affiliate marketing students all of the time who leverage their hobbies and personal interests for income.

Leverage Your Hobbies and Interests

What gets you excited? What do you look forward to doing on your time off? Where do you spend your money in terms of interests and enjoyment? There is a major positive benefit if you decide to leverage your personal interests for affiliate marketing … knowledge.

If you're passionate about something, then you will know more about it than the average person. You'll be able to write informational text about it and help others to understand your excitement and perhaps increase theirs.

When we get into later chapters about websites, blogs, and social media marketing, you'll see that you'll have a huge advantage if you can create original and helpful text about your marketing niche. Especially on the social media sites, you'll be building an audience of friends, contacts, and followers. They will end up in that status because at some point they placed a value on what you have to say.

Once you're talking to those people, they'll tend to place more value on what you say about your niche than on the word of strangers on the Web. This is referral marketing at its best. This is word of mouth that will generate sales and affiliate commissions.

Where do your interests lie?
- games and gaming
- flying airplanes
- flying model airplanes
- fishing or hunting
- gardening
- home improvement
- fitness, exercise, or dieting
- baseball, football, bowling, soccer
- writing
- photography
- cooking
- travel
- hiking
- biking
- horseback riding

There are so many hobbies and areas of interest in which you may be involved. Any or all of them are logical first niche marketing strategies. In case you're drawing a blank, walk around your home and see what magazines you subscribe to or books you've been reading. Those are dead giveaways for your interests. No matter how minor, they're all valuable.

The Bookstore Research Visit

Another way to approach this, if you want to take it from a more third party perspective but you also want to get hints as to market niche opportunities, is to go to the local big box bookstore.

Go to the magazine section first. What section has the greatest number of niche topic magazines and periodicals? It could be computers, photography, food & wine, or others. It's very expensive to publish a glossy magazine these days, so when you see a number of them in one niche, there must be a whole lot of people interested and buying.

Once you've chosen a few topics for a marketing niche, go to the book section and see how many books there are on the same topic. A winner would be a niche with magazines and books addressing everything about the topic.

The image above is the screen of categories on one major affiliate network site. We'll look specifically at that network later, but for now, let's look at these categories as niche markets. Let's look specifically at some of those opportunities.

Things are different at different affiliate networks and with advertisers not in a network, but let's look at some specific examples of actual affiliate linking income potential using this site's measurement, EPC, Earnings Per 100 Clicks. Notice the 3 month and 7 day columns. They indicate the actual dollar conversions from each 100 clicks in that period.

Photography

Advertiser	3 Month EPC (USD)	7 Day EPC (USD)
myphotobook.fr » View Links	$178.23	$31.82
Join Now! $15-$50 CPAs Stamps.com / PhotoStamps.com » View Links	$142.95	$112.78
myphotobook.co.uk » View Links	$139.76	$38.36
Fujicolor Sverige » View Links	$128.84	$51.71
Learn more... CarrotInk.com - Save a Bunch on Printing Supplies » View Links » View Products	$104.13	$42.34
Fujicolor Norway » View Links	$66.45	$5.58
see here by FUJIFILM FUJIFILM SeeHere Partners » View Links » View Products	$66.32	$42.08
Mixbook PHOTO BOOKS · CALENDARS · CARDS Mixbook » View Links	$62.39	$67.09

Remember that most of these only pay if there is a purchase, so if we look at the top result, we see that the average publisher makes $178.23 for every 100 clicks on links to that advertiser's site.

Credit Cards

Advertiser	3 Month EPC (USD)	7 Day EPC (USD)
Orchard Bank MasterCard Affiliate Program » View Links	$171.80	$12.10
DISCOVER CARD Discover Card » View Links	$158.42	$80.48
RushCard » View Links	$41.73	$26.76
UPside Visa Prepaid Card » View Links	$39.50	$107.44
WESTERN UNION moving money for better Western Union: Prepaid Cards » View Links	$37.67	$10.78
Silver Prepaid MasterCard card » View Links	$33.32	$12.23
CreditCards.com » View Links	$30.53	$1.12
CreditExpert from Experian® CreditExpert UK- Free Trial » View Links	$22.10	$26.88

Advertiser	3 Month EPC (USD)	7 Day EPC (USD)
WORKOPOLIS Workopolis - Canada's Biggest Job Site » View Links	$92.10	$106.67
Executive Search Online.com Executive Search Online » View Links	$28.57	$13.10
TheLadders.com » View Links	$27.15	$26.35
6 FIGURE JOBS a Workstream Company 6FigureJobs.com » View Links	$23.44	$28.22
ResumeEdge A @elnet SERVICE EssayEdge.com & ResumeEdge.com » View Links	$15.23	$7.09
Beyond.com Career Network » View Links	$15.01	$11.12

You're beginning to get the idea. Regardless of where your
personal interests lie, there's opportunity. It doesn't matter if
you have no strong interests, since you can find a lot of opportunity by just looking through affiliate network sites.

Affiliate Marketing for Sites & Products You Like

If you're like most of us, you're probably all over the Internet,
and you likely do a lot of online shopping. Online is taking a
gigantic market share away from brick and mortar stores. So
what about checking out the sites where you shop? This can
also tie in with your personal interests and hobbies, since you
buy online for your hobbies, as well.

When you're at a website, check the links and buttons at the
top and especially at the bottom of the page, to see if they
advertise for affiliates.

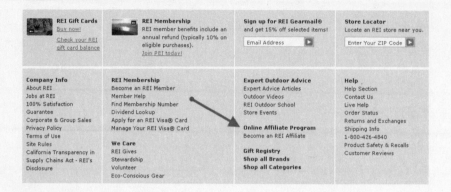

REI.com

The image above is from the bottom of the home page at REI. com. If you're into the outdoors and all of those wonderful products at REI, here's your chance to market for them and make money.

Link	Name	Link ID	3 Month EPC (USD)	7 Day EPC (USD)
Tent Finder at REI Text Link Seasonal Link	10784267 Tent Finder at REI		$145.26	N/A
Check out the online exclusives at RE... Text Link	10548315 REI online only products		$122.44	$36.06
Sale & Clearance Items at REI.com! Sa... Text Link Sale/Discount	10782323 Sale & Clearance Items...		$111.19	$18.67
REI Coupons & Rebates Text Link Coupons	10837179 REI Coupons & Rebates		$99.02	$38.87
Garmin Forerunner 210 GPS at REI Text Link Sale/Discount	10931513 Garmin Forerunner 210 ...		$94.07	N/A
Garmin Oregon 450 GPS at REI Text Link Seasonal Link	10931511 Garmin Oregon 450 GPS ...		$81.20	N/A

Some of the REI links and payouts are shown. These are all text links, but there are plenty of banner ads, too.

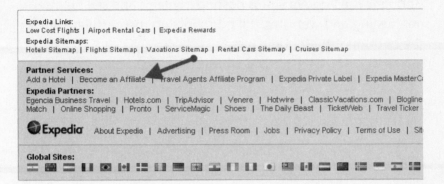

Expedia Links:
Low Cost Flights | Airport Rental Cars | Expedia Rewards
Expedia Sitemaps:
Hotels Sitemap | Flights Sitemap | Vacations Sitemap | Rental Cars Sitemap | Cruises Sitemap

Partner Services:
Add a Hotel | Become an Affiliate | Travel Agents Affiliate Program | Expedia Private Label | Expedia MasterC
Expedia Partners:
Egencia Business Travel | Hotels.com | TripAdvisor | Venere | Hotwire | ClassicVacations.com | Blogline
Match | Online Shopping | Pronto | ServiceMagic | Shoes | The Daily Beast | TicketWeb | Travel Ticker

Expedia   About Expedia | Advertising | Press Room | Jobs | Privacy Policy | Terms of Use | Sit

Global Sites:

Expedia.com

Build Your Business with the Expedia Affiliate Program

Partner with Expedia today and start earning additional revenue for your organization. Our commission-based partnerships allow you to deep-link to worldwide travel products, including:

- Dynamic travel packages (discounted up to 50%)
- More than 140,000 Hotels worldwide
- All major car rental companies in over 20,000 locations
- 300+ airlines

Network Affiliates

Become an affiliate partner and leverage the Expedia brand and offers to monetize your site traffic.

- Quick and easy set up
- Competitive commission rates from the first sale (up to 6%, depending upon the travel products)
- Get 24/7 access to the top Expedia banners, links, and booking engines via Commission Junction, our affiliate network partner

Portals & Meta Search

Develop a partnership with the world's leading travel brand to monetize your site traffic.

- Full content solution
- We sell travel better than anyone else

Go

The bottom of the Expedia.com website also has a link for affiliate marketers that takes them to this page:

GoDaddy.com

GoDaddy is a huge business hosting domains and selling Internet hosting and websites. I'll skip showing their affiliate link at the bottom of their home page.

However, in the next image I'll show you their pitch to affiliates offering up to a 30% commission on sales generated from their websites, blogs, and affiliate activities.

Of course, there's always the good old tried and true Google search. I did one for "highest affiliate commissions" and got thousands of results.

Doing a search like this will require a lot of research, as there are scams in affiliate marketing programs just like anywhere else. High percentage commissions don't always mean high income for the affiliate, either.

A company or advertiser can offer their affiliates 50% or even higher commissions, but if their products don't convert, 50% of nothing is ZERO income. You have to balance your search for the best products and services commission rates with their popularity and ability to convert to commission dollars. Here are the top few free results of that "highest affiliate commissions" search.

Affiliate Marketing – Discover the Best 5 Star **Affiliate** Programs
www.5star**affiliateprogram**s.com/
5 Star **Affiliate** Programs - **Affiliate** Marketing – Best **Affiliate** Programs. Your Leading
Source for **High** Integrity, **High Commission Affiliate** Marketing Programs.
5 Star Affiliate Marketing Forums - Directory - 5 Star Affiliate Blogs - Advertising

Best Paying **Affiliate** Programs - Top Paying **Affiliate Program | High** ...
www.squidoo.com › ... › Internet › Make money online
How many top paying affiliate programs have you come across that is a free affiliate
programme yet only give **high affiliate program** commission when you get.
Why I Called SBI The Best High ... - My Online Experience With SBI ...

Get The **Highest Affiliate Commissions** at Saveology Network
network.saveology.com/**affiliate**-commisions.aspx
SaveologyNetwork offers the **highest affiliate commissions** in the industry for Dish
Network®, ADT®, Protect America, Comcast®, Time Warner Cable, Cox®, ...

AFFILIATE PROGRAMS - The Monster of **Affiliate** Marketing Network
www.**affiliate**bot.com/
High quality wall stickers to decorate your home. Easy to Install and Remove. Free
shipping for order 2 wall stickers. Join the **affiliate program**. Earn 20% ...

Florist One® **Affiliate Program** | The **highest** paying of all florist ...
www.floristone.com/florist-one-**affiliate-program**.cfm
The Florist One **Affiliate Program** is an in-house florist **affiliate program** offering the
highest commissions of any florist **affiliate program**. We offer generous ...

Website **Affiliate Program - Highest Commissions** - Payouts
www.commercialloandirect.com › Affiliates & Referrals
Affiliates and referrals for webmasters and website owners **program** by Commercial
Loan Direct - join one of the best paid programs on the internet.

That's a broad-brush approach to searching for affiliate pro-
grams, but you can be more targeted by searching on the niche
and the word "affiliate" or the key phrase "affiliate program."
As an example, I did a Google search on "camping supply affili-
ate program" and turned up some great companies:
• Camping Gear Outlet.com
• Bentgear
• Cabela's
• Bass Pro Shops
• BackCountry.com
There were more, and this is a great way to quickly get to their
affiliate program page, as that's where the key phrase search
frequently points. If you end up on the home page, just go to
the bottom and look for an affiliates or affiliate program link.
You can even end up on sites that are affiliates for affiliate pro-
grams! I did a Google search on fitness affiliate programs and

found many, but one was a site pointing me to others:

Program name		Commission
	www.achieve-fitness.com **Sign up here** Personal trainers in Maryland, DC, and Northern Virginia - Personal Fitness Training in Bethesda, Potomoac, Rockville, Gaithersburg, Germantown Maryland Affiliate info »	CPS 40.0%
	www.gamecycles.com **Sign up here** GameCycles - Making Fitness Fun. We carry Cateye GameBikes, GameBike Pro, Gamercycle, NeoRacer DDR (Dance Dance Revolution products) and Island Worlds. Affiliate info »	CPS 5.0%
	www.demandfitness.com **Sign up here** Online fitness classes, accessible anytime, anywhere! demandFITNESS is your fitness on demand solution that uses the Internet to deliver: convenient weight loss exercise at home, easy to follow home ... Affiliate info »	CPS 10.0%
	www.onlinefitnesslog.com **Sign up here** Healthy eating and exercise can also help you look and feel younger, reduce the affects of aging, and live a longer, fuller life. Now, who wouldn?t want that? As if all of that wasn?t enough, studies ... Affiliate info »	CPS 20.0%
	www.crosstrainer.ca **Sign up here** Crosstrainer - The leading fitness, exercise, nutrition and weight loss software program on the market. Try it for free. Its complete and thorough set of easy-to-use features are designed for ... Affiliate info »	CPS 45.0%
	www.afan.com.au **Sign up here** Australia discount supplements : - Acetyl L-Carnitine Amino Acids Carbohydrate Polymers Cartilage Repair Colostrum Creatine (All types) Creatine Stacks Endurance HMB Weight Loss L-Carnitine ... Affiliate info »	CPS 5.0%

It's clear that you'll have no trouble in locating a great many affiliate programs in almost any niche in which you want to specialize. The trick is to evaluate them for their income potential, not just the payout commission percentage, but the conversion rate. I'd rather get paid 5% to convert 30% of clicks to a sale than get 15% from a site that only manages to convert 5% of clicks.

You can see that there is nothing but opportunity in front of you, and the next chapter is going to be even more exciting. Information products pay the highest commissions on the Web, and I'll show you how to get your share of that action.

CHAPTER 4

Information Products for High Commissions

You're holding this book, with covers and nice trimmed paper pages, and it's a substantial and solid thing. Many people will never get away from paper books, and they will always have bookshelves with stacks of them. I want you to be able to pick this book off the shelf and go to the right page where you can refresh your memory about the best affiliate marketing solutions.

However, digital information products are a huge and rapidly expanding business on the Internet. Sure, we kill fewer trees when we don't print a book on paper, but it's not nearly as much about the environment as it is about convenience and speed of delivery. It certainly doesn't hurt that you can carry around a hundred or more books in a tiny electronic device when it would take a truck to carry the same number of books in print.

The image at the beginning of this chapter is of an eBook, but don't narrow your focus and assume that an eBook must have a certain number of pages or have a table of contents and an index to be an "eBook." A simple PDF document can be called an eBook, and there are a great many of them out there, many with fewer than a dozen pages.

You see, the "information product" can be delivered in print as well, or on a CD Rom, or on a DVD. Many are delivered that way, but far more of them are delivered electronically as digital products. It's these digital formats and inexpensive disks that provide one of the greatest opportunities for authors and affiliate marketers. It's the low cost of production that is lucrative.

Yes, a DVD must be produced, and that's one reason that the format is dropping in popularity in comparison to digital files and eBooks. There is no inventory requirement, and there is no production expense. Once it's written and ready to sell, it's a file on a disk or server. That file can be sold tens of thousands of times without any other costs, either for production or for delivery.

So open your mind to accept a number of digital product formats and delivery mechanisms, and you'll open your business to more opportunity. There are even information products that deliver nothing other than a login to a protected site available only to paying customers. The customer pays an ongoing membership fee and gets access to the information they want by logging in and using the website or forum.

Amazon sold more eBooks than print books in 2011. In April of 2011, Amazon.com announced that the online store had seen the sale of eBooks surpass print copies in March. That was a major milestone and the media reported it extensively. Recent numbers indicate eBooks selling at a rate of two to one over books in print.

It's eBooks, Reports, White Papers and More

When we talk about digital information products here, we could be talking about an eBook, a "special report," or even a "how-to guide." They're simply information products delivered in digital form to be consumed/read on a computer, cell phone, tablet, or eReading device.

Whatever you call the digital file that's delivered, and no matter what mechanism or network it's delivered through, I'm going to show you how affiliate marketers are making a great deal of money helping these digital information product authors to sell their information on the Web.

What & Why Do People Buy Information Products?

While people do buy many online digital products on a whim or as an impulse purchase, many are also out there searching for the right information to improve their lives in some way. They may be looking for fitness information and exercise programs to improve their health, diet plans to lose weight, or for any other personal self-improvement goal.

Business people, or those who want to start a business, search for information about opportunities and how to get started. People look for information for a happier lifestyle, including books and reports about food, wine, healthy eating, travel, and every hobby you can think of. All of the information I gave you about products and services in previous chapters applies to niche marketing of information products, as well. If there are people reading books and magazines about a hobby or interest, they're also buying information products about it.

Is every report, eBook, or digital information product a good one? Just like hard products, some are good, some aren't, some sell really well, and others don't. However, the theme of this chapter is that choosing information products as an affiliate marketing strategy can yield the highest percentage commissions of any other type of product or service out there.

Scams & Quality Are a Concern
Xxxxxxxxxxxxx **ADD PHOTO HERE** xxxxxxxxxxxxxxx
Let's look at what it takes to produce a digital information product.

- A computer
- An idea and title

That's pretty much it. You don't really have to be an expert about nutrition to author a report on the best diet supplement. You don't even have to know a thing about it at all because there is no real cost involved in authoring digital products, anyone can do it, and many are doing it who shouldn't be.

Of course there is great digital material out there that you can promote as an affiliate and that will allow you to make good money and be proud of the products. However, it's going to take a little more effort up front on your part to make sure that you select products that are as they're advertised, and that provide value for the customer. This is particularly true when many of the information products you'll be promoting are about self-improvement or making money. People are searching for better lives, and you want to promote information that actually helps them to achieve their goals.

So How Does It Work?
Just as you do with the regular products in previous chapters, you place links and ads in websites, blogs, and on the social media that promote specific digital information products. When

someone clicks on one of your ads and makes a purchase, you get paid. The process is handled in much the same way as it is for products and services, only the product in this case is normally delivered immediately at purchase as a downloadable file. You can work directly with authors or through small niche-focused publishing and delivery networks, but the largest number of affiliate marketers who specialize in information products are still using one major network, ClickBank.com.

ClickBank is a huge site that matches up affiliate marketers with authors of digital information products and eBooks. You'll be able to locate other networks providing similar services, such as PayDotCom, but ClickBank is the largest, so I'll use it as our example and instructional resource.

ClickBank for Affiliate Profits

I wanted to start out by showing the image with the ClickBank major categories. It clearly illustrates the variety and breadth of material and subject matter available to the affiliate marketer to promote and earn commissions.

If you want to start with your own hobbies or interests, you'll find information products to promote. Or just decide on one or more niche topic and jump right in.

You'll be doing many of the same things that you do for hard products and services:
- posting about them on websites
- blogging about them
- discussing them on social networks

What I want to do in this chapter is give you a thorough over-view of how this process works using ClickBank, and much of the information here is available in their Affiliate help pages on the website.

We're approaching this as a business, but I like ClickBank's an-swer to their help question about "what is an affiliate?" They use an individual who is an avid gardener. Call her Judy. Judy buys a great eBook that helps them to grow larger and more beautiful roses.

Judy really appreciates the help she received from the eBook, and she mentions it and links to it in various social network gardening and rose groups. Those are free advertising posts for the eBook, but Judy is missing an opportunity. She can sign up free as an affiliate at ClickBank and get what they call a "Hop-link" to use in the future when she recommends the eBook. Then she gets paid.

This example focuses on using your own interests or hobby to generate income, which is a great place to start. If you're already talking to others on the Web about common interests, look first for information products that are in that niche and you'll have a head-start on profits.

Buy it First
You don't have to follow this advice, but you might want to make it a quality assurance part of your marketing process. Before you promote an information product, buy it and read it yourself. If you feel like you received value that was worth the price you paid, then promote it. If not, move on to something better.

Though ClickBank itself states that you don't have to purchase the products to promote them, the site does say that doing so can give you fresh ideas about how to promote the product for better results. An example from the Judy gardening story might be that a single helpful tip learned in the eBook increased the growth rate of her flowers. Knowing what's in the product creates marketing opportunities.

ClickBank Dos and Don'ts

Clickbank has a page of best practices and things you should avoid as an affiliate, and I'll share a few of the bullet points with you here:

Dos
- promote high quality products
- use techniques/strategies recommended by the author or vendor, since they know what sells
- monitor results and be willing to make changes to increase sales
- choose an account nickname you won't mind others seeing, as it's coded into your Hoplinks

Don'ts
- don't spam...anywhere
- don't use negative advertising campaigns, as many vendors don't like this approach
- don't over-expect results; it takes time to build an income from information products
- These are some of the highlights worth keeping in mind as you set up your affiliate account and begin your marketing through ClickBank.

Measurement Options and Sorting

ClickBank uses several measurements or performance calculations to indicate a product's sales and income potential. Before we do some searches for products, we'll want to understand these, as we can use them to sort our results so that we see at the top of the display the best products for our purposes.

High – Low Gravity

You can sort results by "gravity," high > low, or the reverse. Gravity refers to the number of affiliates who have actually earned a commission promoting a particular product. If a publisher has a high Gravity Score, it means that there have been many affiliates earning commissions from promoting that product. Low Gravity means just the opposite.

Usually affiliates will want to search for products with high gravity scores because it means that the product sells well. However, this also usually means that there's a lot more competition, with many affiliates promoting the product around the Web. Sometimes searching for newer products with low gravity scores can yield a "diamond in the rough" that other marketers haven't yet discovered.

Initial $/Sale

Later in the book when we talk about Search Engine Marketing, SEM, and paying for ad placement, you'll see the value in this search sort criteria. This is the amount of money made on the sale of the product.

If you're paying for clicks or advertising, you'll need to know two things: how many clicks on average will convert to a purchase, and second, how much each purchase ends up costing you. So if you're paying $0.25/click to advertise a certain information product, and your stats show that one out of every 50 clicks makes a purchase, you're paying $12.50 for each purchase.

Now you know what it costs for one product sale, so when

you search for a product to promote, you'll probably indicate you want those with an Initial $/Sale of $25.00 or more to the affiliate.

Avg %/Sale

This ranks the items in the search results by the average percentage paid by the vendor. If you're looking for high commission percentages, this is the way to bring them to the top of your search.

Avg Rebill Total and Avg $/Sale

Many of the products sold through ClickBank are recurring subscription products. This means that the customer is paying more than once, maybe even monthly, for a subscription, or in some other way paying into the future. As an affiliate, you can earn a percentage of that future income. Using this search criteria, you can search for these type of products by rebill amounts and frequency.

Now you know how other affiliates are using their ClickBank searches to locate products and evaluate them for their promotional purposes.

Search for "Dietary Supplement"

Let's get started with some examples of product niche searches and how products are located and evaluated on ClickBank. We'll do several across different product niches to give you a firm foundation in how to get your HopLinks to begin promoting products.

This first search is on the keywords "dietary supplement," as the image below shows. In this case I chose to only place a minimum Gravity Score qualifier. I chose 150 as the minimum score, as there are vendors with scores this high, and I want to see products that really sell.

Advanced Search		
Enter Keywords:	dietary supplement	
Exclude words from search:		
In this Category:	- All categories -	
Results per page:	10	
		Search Reset

Stats

Gravity
☑ Show items with gravity: | Higher than | 150

Initial $/sale
☐ Show items with initial $/sale: | Higher than | |

Avg $/sale
☐ Show items with avg $/sale: | Higher than | |

Avg Rebill Total
☐ Show items with Avg Rebill Total: | Higher than | |

Avg %/sale
☐ Show items with avg %/sale: | Higher than | |

Avg %/rebill
☐ Show items with avg %/rebill: | Higher than | |

I could select other criteria, such as the Initial $/Sale, but right now I just want to see one or more products with a high gravity score indicating that there are a lot of affiliates making money with the product. Here is the top result for this search:

Results   Marketplace Help

Displaying results 1-2 out of 2 (pg. 1 of 1)

Results per page: 10 ▾

Sort results by:
Keyword Relevance ▾

Burn The Fat, Feed The Muscle: Pays Out Up   Avg $/sale
To $86 $25.59
Others Come And Go. Burn The Fat Has Been A
Perennial Bestseller Since 2002. New 1 Click   Promote
Upsell Brings Your Payout As High As $86 Per
Customer. Get Your Affiliate Tools At: ☆
Burnthefat.com/affiliates   Add To Bookmarks

Stats: Initial $/sale: $22.37 | Avg %/sale: 60.0% |
Avg Rebill Total: $17.66 | Avg %/rebill: 60.0% | Grav: 159.61
Cat: **Health & Fitness : Diets & Weight Loss**

My Stats: No data found for this vendor in the selected time
period.

Like 2k

There's a lot of information here. The description indicates that
"Burn the Fat, Feed the Muscle" has been around since 2002,
and as a bonus it has some upsell potential to other products
that will pay you again as an affiliate after the first sale. Other
information:

- Initial $/Sale is $22.37.
- Commission percentage averages 60%.
- Avg Rebill Total is $17.66, with a commission percent-
  age again of 60%.

From what we know now, we can assume that this product has
had a lot of exposure for around 10 years, so we could have a
competitive uphill battle. Or it could be close to a saturation
point in certain markets, especially in certain age groups. So we
might want to target younger age groups with our marketing

when we can, as they may not have yet seen the product. We know what we'll make from each sale, and we may have some data from other related products we're promoting to help us figure out a conservative conversion rate for clicks. Of course, as long as you're not doing paid marketing, or paying for ads or clicks, it's all profit.

You just write articles and posts on social media about it and place the HopLink. Conversion rate is always important, but if you're not paying for the exposure, every click is potential income without cost risk.

Flight Simulator Game

I did a search on "model airplane," but this turned up and was interesting:

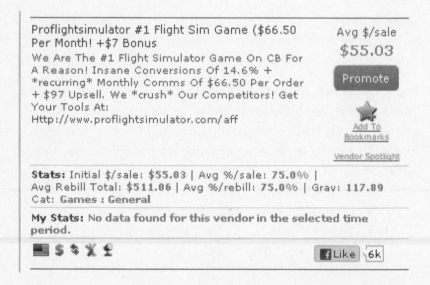

This is actually game software, but it sells well. Note that the Initial $/Sale is $55.03, but the Avg Rebill Total is a whopping $511.86 due to the monthly recurring billing. If you're promoting games and gaming, this could be a great product for you.

Here's another approach that will work well if you're blogging about RVs, camping with an RV, and gear. It will also work well with Facebook fan pages or Google+ business pages focused on this topic and directed to avid RV fans.

You can pick up many publications, none of which are a whole lot of money individually, that are a great way to provide more informational resources for your fans and readers.
Just place these links in your articles and posts.

When I talk later about blogging or Facebook and Google+ pages focused on a market niche, you'll see how you can combine information products like these with selling regular products and services. Your site or page becomes a resource and a destination to talk about RVs and the RV lifestyle.

Climb on the "Green" Movement

Everybody's trying to go "green" in some way or another. We all care about our planet and our air and water. There is a lot of opportunity to appeal to an audience of potential customers who are passionate about this niche, and many are affluent enough to buy whatever products or information material you can promote.

The image above was the top couple of items from a marketplace search without any keywords, only the Category Green Products and a minimum gravity score of 100.

Notice that the top result also has recurring or future rebill amounts. The payout is 74% of sale amount, so this could be a great thing to write about in your blog or on your social media niche-focused pages.

I did another search with no keywords on the Home & Garden category and turned up these two woodworking results. These are great products to promote on sites popular with men and do-it-yourselfers. If you're blogging about home projects and home improvements, these are great information products that will get good click-through action.

The link from the title of all of these ad promos is to the landing page where the prospect is taken from your HopLink. You should visit the page and see how it presents the product and see how you would respond to it. If you're turned off by the ad or you wouldn't make a purchase even if you have an interest, then you might want to search for a better one.

Don't place too much concentration on past ad performance in your evaluation. If you would respond to the ad, low numbers historically could just mean others didn't promote it well. Go with your instincts and promote products that you like and would buy.

ClickBank Promotional Tools

You're going to be doing all of the things I'm presenting to you in this book in order to promote your ClickBank information products. Some of those venues will involve blogging and, of course, the social networks. There are a few tools that Click-Bank provides to help.

WordPress
When I tell you about blogging, I'll lean heavily on using Word-Press, as it's a very strong and popular platform. It's so popular that it's the only platform for which ClickBank provides plugin enhancements.

Two plugins help the user to easily integrate HopLinks into their WordPress site and to protect downloaded material from plagiarism and unauthorized copying and resale.

SocialPromote
This is a ClickBank proprietary tool to promote products on Facebook. It's so easy you can't afford not to use it. When you're logged into ClickBank, you'll see a "Like" button next to the products. When you click that button, the product link will automatically display in your Facebook account and your Friends will see it in their News Feed.

Reporting and Analytics

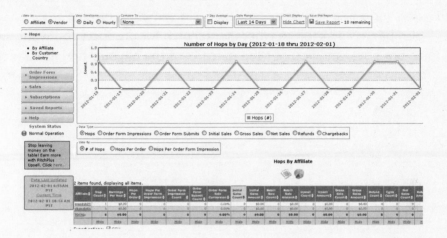

The image above is a sample for the screen where you can track the performance of your HopLinks and where your income is coming from. As with all affiliate marketing, the more you track and analyze, the more you can do to improve your results and increase your profits.

Especially when you're promoting in the social media, you're going to be building a reputation for reliability and trust. If you allow poorly-performing links or low quality products to stay on your pages, your reputation could suffer and your sales suffer with it.

e-Junkie.com

e-Junkie.com is another site for affiliates to market digital products, including software, music, and information products. It also has a Marketplace where you search for products you want to promote, and you get the specifics of the payouts and links

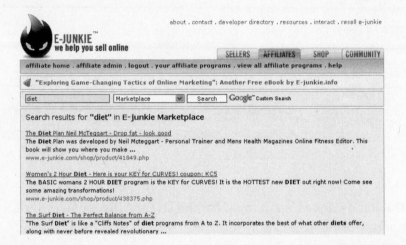

to the vendor promotion pages.

The image above shows a search in the Marketplace on the term "diet." I just grabbed the first product and clicked to see what it was about. I found that it pays a 10% commission, and then I signed up and went to the page to get the link to pro-

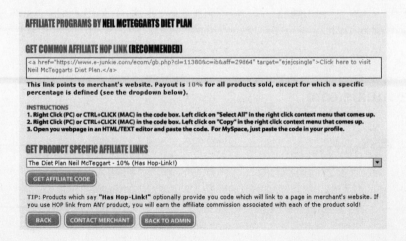

mote it.

You'll find that many information product vendors will sign up with several affiliate networks, so you may just work with one, or you could sign up with several.

You may decide not to promote information products, however they can present a great opportunity to educate your site visitors while making money. And they'll present more balanced offerings and site content when you're working a niche site, blog, or social media page.

CHAPTER 5

Affiliate Networks –
Commission Junction

Commission Junction is a company that handles affiliate marketing programs for advertising agencies, companies, and vendors on a large scale. The management tasks for maintaining an affiliate network, as well as the costs, create a demand for the services of this company.

Advertisers (our customers) and Publishers (us) sign up with CJ to connect. Commission Junction handles all of the details of the relationship, including monitoring the many hundreds of thousands of links and ads, their performance, and then paying the affiliates appropriately.

You sign up free for an account at CJ.com, and you'll immediately be given access to thousands of companies and hundreds of thousands of ads and links for profitable promotions.

You Have to Qualify

Before you jump into Commission Junction's searches for advertisers, you need to know that you must apply to market the products and services individually with each company. It's just a few clicks, as CJ handles that part. However, approval isn't a slam-dunk process.

Some advertisers will accept you almost immediately without a check of any kind. However, many of them are going to want to check out the sites where you'll be marketing their products. If they don't believe that your marketing venues will bring them sufficient business, you'll get turned down.

When you set up your CJ account, you enter information, including sites that you own and use for marketing. You'll also give an overview of how you market and where, including social media. Doing so gives the advertisers something to go on when they're deciding whether to accept you as an affiliate. So have your business plan, website(s), and blog(s) up and running before you try to apply to too many advertisers on this network. As I said, some will just approve you without a look, so you can get started right away, but be prepared for rejection in some cases.

Let's run through some of the many categories of advertisers and products, as well as look at how you can make decisions about which ones you want to promote.

Example Product & Link Strategies

Advertiser	3 Month EPC (USD)	7 Day EPC (USD)
☐ SmoothFitness.com » View Links » View Products	$163.60	$122.29
☐ PRO-FORM ProForm & WorkoutWarehouse by ICON Health & Fitness » View Links » View Products	$70.55	$48.03
☐ LIVE STRONG FITNESS » View Links » View Products	$67.31	$57.35
☐ 24 FITNESS 24 Hour Fitness » View Links » View Products	$32.02	$21.95
☐ Bally Total Fitness » View Links	$12.56	$0.00
☐ Tony Little-America's Personal Trainer-Products » View Links	$3.73	$4.10

Fitness Products

The image shows the result of an "Advertiser" search in CJ for the keyword "fitness." This turns up actual companies and advertisers, not specific links. Taking the top one on the list and clicking the "View Links" link, we get the display in the next image.

Link	Name	Link ID	3 Month EPC (USD)	7 Day EPC (USD)
Save $100 on the Smooth Agile DMT X2 ... Text Link Coupons	10279731 Save $100 on the Agile...		$562.48	N/A
The Smooth 5.65 Folding Treadmill Text Link Hot Product	10864706 New Smooth 5.65 Treadm...		$412.74	$113.42
Lose Weight and Get in Shape – ... Text Link	5340788 Lose Weight and Get in...		$337.03	N/A
160x600 Wide Skyscraper Sale/Discount	10842287 5% Off Any Smooth Trea...		$307.36	N/A

Back in Chapter 3, I explained the EPC, Earnings Per 100 Clicks columns, which help you make decisions about which advertisers and products to promote. In the previous image, we find specific product and promotional links and advertising banners. Taking the second link to the product page for the treadmill, we find that it sells on that page for $999. With a commission percentage for this company's items between 8% and 12%, you can see that there is some money to be made if you can get people to click through and buy this company's equipment.

Camping Equipment

Advertiser	3 Month EPC (USD)	7 Day EPC (USD)	Network Earnings	Sale	Lead	Clic
Outdoor Megastore » View Links	$14.88	$5.71		Sale: 10.00% GBP		
Sunny Sports » View Links » View Products	$54.87	$20.04		Sale: 5.00% - 6.00% USD		
Moosejaw » View Links » View Products	$45.33	$59.33		Sale: 8.00% USD Performance Incentive		
Skis.com » View Links » View Products	$15.64	$34.10		Sale: 8.00% USD		
Paragon Sports » View Links » View Products	$14.72	$17.18		Sale: 8.00% USD Performance Incentive		
Government Military Surplus Auctions » View Links	$4.39	$1.39		Sale: 1.00% USD Lead: $0.10 - $1.00 USD		
Online Sports » View Links » View Products	$3.66	$0.72		Sale: 10.00% USD Performance Incentive		
eagleoptics.com » View Links	$60.44	$49.69		Sale: 5.00% USD		
Department of Goods » View Links » View Products	$55.23	$28.87		Sale: 5.00% USD		

In this "camping equipment" search, we want to look at Moosejaw to see if there is opportunity with this vendor. First, by clicking on the link to the company at the left under the image, we get a page with a description of the company and its products. Here's what they have to say about themselves:

Category: Outdoors *(show similar advertisers)*

Description: Moosejaw - one of the fastest growing outdoor retailer in the country - offers mid to high-end mountain apparel and outdoor equipment. We have been recognized for outstanding business practices by the New York Times, Chicago Tribune, Business Week SB and Entrepreneur Magazine. We carry over 8,000 products from The North Face, Arcteryx, Patagonia, Marmot, Mountain Hardwear and much more. Moosejaw.com has cutting edge navigation, top of the line zoom functionality, competitive prices and a unique brand of silliness that breeds unparalleled loyalty. Your customers automatically get Moosejaw Rewards Points (10% toward moosejawrewards.com on regular price items, 5% sale price items) on every purchase. It is free and it gives us a huge advantage over the competition. Finally, Moosejaw shocks its customers with amazing service and with 120 day cookies for affiliates, you will benefit too!

With this information, and the knowledge that we're building a pretty good following at our outdoors blog and Facebook and Google+ pages about outdoor activities, we decide to look at a link or two.

Link	Name	Link ID	3 Month EPC (USD)	7 Day EPC (USD)	Sale	Lead	Click
5% off Sale Merchandise with coupon c... Text Link Coupons	10663264 5% off Sale Merchandis...		$130.19	$65.08	Sale: 8.00% USD Performance Incentive		
Moosejaw 88x31 Micro Bar	10385636 Moosejaw Logo		$125.64	$145.56	Sale: 8.00% USD Performance Incentive		
Moosejaw 88x31 Micro Bar	10394757 Funky Logo		$118.60	$90.01	Sale: 8.00% USD Performance Incentive		

The first link in the display mentions coupons, so let's take a look at the page displayed when we click that Text Link Coupons link:

Link Detail

5% off Sale Merchandise with coupon code CJSALE	
Link Status	Active
Promotional Dates	1-Dec-2011 - 30-Dec-2012
Link ID/Name	10663264 / 5% off Sale Merchandise with coupon code CJSALE
Link Type/Size	Text Link Coupons
Description	5% off Sale Merchandise any time with coupon code CJSALE. Exclusions include: Yakima, Burton, Volcom, Liquid Force, Foursquare, Analog, Sessions, Oakley, Camelbak, and other Select Snow/Wake/Skate brands.
Link Designation	JavaScript and HTML Available
Destination	View Destination Page Advertiser allows URL redirects for this link.
3 Month EPC	$130.19 USD
7 Day EPC	$65.08 USD
Advertiser	Moosejaw
Category	Recreation & Leisure > Outdoors
Link Language	English

This page gives the detail of the link offer. The visitor gets a 5% off coupon code for purchases. From the previous image, we see that we get 8% for a commission, so this may be a good company to promote if we have the right sites and exposure to do so.

Advertiser	3 Month EPC (USD)	7 Day EPC (USD)	Network Earnings	Sale	Lea
WorldWinner WorldWinner.com Online Games for Cash Prizes » View Links	$36.59	$30.58		Sale: $30.00 USD Lead: $1.50 USD Performance Incentive	
GameHouse GameHouse » View Links » View Products	$25.35	$11.06		Lead: $15.00 USD	

Games

In a search on "games," I found plenty of advertiser results. Looking at the second one at the arrow, we find that this advertiser pays for leads, not just sales.

As the worldwide leader in casual games, GameHouse makes it easy to profit and be a part of the fast-growing and extremely popular download-able games business. Casual gaming is the fastest growing segment of the PC market and GameHouse is the **highest-paying** casual games affiliate program on the Web.

Payouts **start at $15** for each 30-day Free trial sign up of FunTicket. With the FunTicket trial, your users can immediately choose one Free full-version game (a $20 value) to own forever!

Payouts for FunPass **start at $20** for each 7-day Free trial sign up of FunPass. With the GameHouse FunPass trial, your users can have unlimited access to over 900 games any time and can purchase games at 65% off retail!

This could be a really great advertiser to promote, especially if you're active on sites and blogs about games and online gaming. There are two Free Trial offers, one a 30 day trial with a $15 commission to the affiliate and the other a 7 day trial with a $20 commission.

Audio Books

Actually, the search I did was on "ebook," but I found Audible. com and it helps to illustrate that there are also digitally deliv-

Advertiser	3 Month EPC (USD)	7 Day EPC (USD)	Network Earnings	Sale	Lead
Primal Nutrition » View Links	$67.79	$43.06		Sale: 30.00% USD Performance Incentive	
$25 Commissions	$52.60	$38.51		Sale: 10.00% USD Lead: $10.00 - $25.00 USD	
Audible.com » View Links » View Products					

ered products on CJ.com.

Their flashing banner shows $25 commissions, and they show a 10% commission rate. The EPC numbers look good too. Audible.com provides digital delivery of audio books, magazines, and newspapers. They also have another type of link that other advertisers use as well, and it's a great one for affiliate marketers who want to target products on a site.

With this type of site and with electronic products sites, there are a huge number of products, and sometimes you can lose a commission simply because the visitor from your click grew tired of looking before they found what they wanted. However, using an "Advanced Link," you can target specific products or product categories.

An Advanced Link is one that you customize based on the product or category you want to target. Let's say you're affiliate marketing for a huge electronics website, but you're writing an article about the benefits of the all-in-one printer/scanner/fax machines. You aren't pushing a brand, just a type of equipment. You can go to the page on the advertiser's site where they display these printers by brand and use the URL address for that page to create an Advanced Link.

Now you write your article about your great experience in your home office using an all-in-one printer, and you may tell them the brand and model you use. However, you tell your readers that their needs may be different from yours, so here's a link to some great all-in-one printers by brand. Your link will take them directly to that page, but it will make sure you get paid with your affiliate code in the Advanced Link.

Commission Junction SmartZones

Another feature offered by Commission Junction is SmartZones. The more brands and advertisers you promote, the more links and ads you'll be running. Particularly when you're placing them on your own websites and blogs, you'll find that offers expire, ads cease to function, and you just may want to try another offer to see if it works better. The CJ SmartZones feature makes it a lot easier to do and saves you a ton of time.

Basically, let's say that you have a blog in the fitness niche. You have a number of banner ads and links running in the sidebars of the blog, particularly next to relevant content in posts and pages. By setting up a SmartZone, you can change and rotate those ads from inside your Commission Junction publisher account manager.

CJ Pay-Per-Call

Before this approach to affiliate marketing, advertisers were hampered in their marketing when they could do a better job through a phone conversation between their sales staff and the prospect.

CJ has created a new marketing approach that provides affiliate marketers with a special phone number to promote instead of a link. The publisher, that's us, creates and promotes ads with these special phone numbers, and they are tracked just like an affiliate link to get the affiliate paid appropriately.
Using this type of marketing, advertisers can add more high ticket products and services to their affiliate marketing network. These higher end items require a more one-on-one consultative sales approach. When the affiliate marketer advertises the phone number, the advertiser's staff answers and takes over the sale process.

Some of these Pay-Per-Call promotions may pay just for getting the caller to connect, though there will be time minimums to guarantee that it wasn't a wrong number or fake call. The advertiser sets the rules, and they may pay just for the call or for a sale that results from the call. There may be a base payout for the call and a bonus if there is a purchase or other action taken by the caller.

One major advantage of this type of affiliate marketing will be the ability to place it in mobile marketing campaigns. Phone numbers in mobile phone marketing are normally "hot" like links. The mobile recipient sees the promotional message and the number, and they can simply tap on it to be connected. It's the ultimate in impulse marketing.

There are a whole lot of affiliate marketers connecting with major advertisers using Commission Junction, so give it a look.

CHAPTER 6

Affiliate Networks – Linkshare

Linkshare consistently ranks as one of the largest affiliate networks on the Web. In fact, just the week before I was writing this, Linkshare was voted the top affiliate network by mthink.com. Here's what the site had to say about arriving at that endorsement:

"LinkShare has earned this year's top spot based on the strength of its platform, the quality of its support, and its overall commitment to driving revenue and commissions through the online channel," said Chris Trayhorn, CEO of mThink. "While the top 20 performance marketing networks are presented by mThink, the results are derived from the survey as well as our esteemed Blue Ribbon Panel of unbiased, third party judges that span every aspect of the online marketing community."

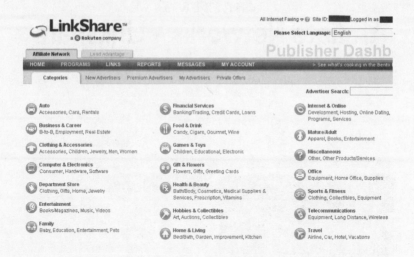

Since you've been through the Commission Junction chapter, I won't have to go into a lot of basic instruction about how the affiliate network operates. The image above shows the categories listed at LinkShare for locating affiliate advertisers and links to promote. LinkShare when I wrote this was showing 788 advertisers spread across these categories.

Private Links

LinkShare works pretty much like Commission Junction does, in that you as an affiliate marketer build relationships with advertisers and market their products and services on your websites, blogs and social media accounts. One thing a bit unique about LinkShare is the "Private Links" feature. Based on your website or blog subject matter, advertisers, may invite you to a relationship.

The image above shows an invitation for private linking from a discount airline fare and hotel booking service. It was received by an affiliate marketer with a blog that related specifically to travel and vacation spots.

Their program description page shows their flat rate commissions for flight, hotel, car rental, or vacation bookings. They also provide a 90 day cookie. This is very important because many times people take awhile to plan a vacation, and they may visit the site multiple times and shop around before purchasing. This gives your link 90 days to create income from their first click and visit.

The image above is the top result in a quick search by category on "clothing."

This vendor is advertising a 25% commission:

Welcome To Our Affiliate Program!

365 Days Offer: 50% to 75% off on Entire Site 'ONLY' thru Affiliates!

If you love shoes and fashion then you are the right person for Shoe Scandal's affiliate program.

ShoeScandal is offering an exciting affiliate program across the USA that pays you cash for referring customers to our site! Earn 25% commission for each sale you refer! HIGHEST Commission in the Retail Footwear & Fashion Industry! ShoeScandal will provide you with a Banner Add 'or' Text Links to upload to your site, Facebook page, Twitter or your Email-Lists.

Simply, just copy and paste the ad or links to your blog, website or email, and track the sales you originate through your affiliate account. It's that simple! An average order of $100 can help you earn $25 per order!

With the cost of ladies' clothing, 25% in commission can mean a nice chunk of change for each purchase. Here are some sample links provided for this company for website or email use:

Link	Link Type	Start Date
ShoeScandal Savings $78! Buy Now! (6) Australian Winter Boots! This Season's Biggest Blowout Sale of 75% Discounts! $22 only! Original $100, Total Savings $78! Buy Now!	Text / Email	01-25-2012
ShoeScandal Faux-Shearing Winter Boots (7) Faux-Shearing Winter Boots at 75% Discount! This Season's Famous Foot Warmer! Shop Now!	Text / Email	01-25-2012
ShoeScandal Classic Australian Winter Boots! (8) Classic Australian Winter Boots! Faux-Fur gives you the warmth and style you desire this winter! At 75% Discount! Only for a Limited Time $22 Only! Buy Now!	Text / Email	01-25-2012
ShoeScandal Three Button Boots! Classic Tall! (9) Three Button Boots! Classic Tall! Classic Short! Single Button Boots! Every Woman's Dream of having these Classic Winter Boots! Shop Now only for a limited time at 75% SALE!	Text / Email	01-25-2012

I did another search on the category and sub-category Sports & Fitness > Equipment. I found this company among many others:

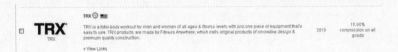

TRX provides equipment and products related to physical fitness and exercise. Their commission is 15%, and their average sale is stated to be $200, as shown at their affiliate information and sign-up page.

Notice also that they provide a 45 day cookie, so the visitor has some time to think about it, as well as setting the affiliate up for more income if they return within 45 days and purchase again.

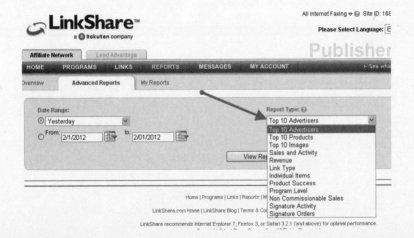

As far as reporting and tracking your results, Linkshare provides a suite of detailed reports, as seen in the image above. Track by product and link, and keep up with detailed revenue and sales statistics.

Now you have information on two of the largest affiliate networks, Commission Junction and Linkshare. They're both fine networks, and you'll make a ton of money as an affiliate marketer using their services. In the next chapter, we'll look at other networks, most not as large, and some very niche-focused.

CHAPTER 7

Other Affiliate Networks

Affiliate marketing is all about worlds. There is the World Wide Web, the marketing platform that exposes our advertising to everyone using it around the world. However, affiliate marketing is also made up of smaller affiliate-focused and niche-targeted networks specializing in connecting advertisers and publishers.

These networks, like Commission Junction, can be broad in the niche markets they serve. They have all types of product and service categories. Or a network can be more focused, serving a specific niche, like some I'll tell you about in this chapter. There are "green" affiliate networks, travel affiliate networks, health affiliate networks, and many more.

I'm not making any specific recommendations in this chapter. My goal is to present a few of the many choices you'll find for your business and to illustrate the niche focus of some networks. I'll give you some basic information about each, and you may find some you want to investigate further.

Advertising.com

At their page for recruiting publishers, Advertising.com states that the site offers 91 of the top 100 advertisers listed by Ad Age. They monetize nearly 1.5 billion impressions every day.

ClixGalore.com

Affiliates / Publishers	New Merchant Programs		Rate	Type
Join Free Now!	ebeautyusa	2 Tier	(US$)10.0%	% Per Sale
Sign Up - click here	Free Brokerage and Investment Education		US$0.50	Per Lead
Affiliates, turn your valuable web site traffic into money now by joining Affiliate programs and driving customers to the many thousands of Merchants using the clixGalore Affiliate Marketing network to advertise their business. Start earning commission now for the sales you generate for our Merchants. You may promote our Merchants using both text or graphic advertisements, including the many	The Homeworker		US$5.00	Per Sale
	BELDT Labs	2 Tier	US$4.62	Per Sale
	Bondi - Hang it on!	2 Tier	(US$)10.0%	% Per Sale
	Deep Cello Coffee Roasters	2 Tier	(US$)10.0%	% Per Sale
	India Emporium		(US$)10.0%	% Per Sale
	Best Travel Card - Pick a gold travel card		US$12.00	Per Sale
	Wedding-now.com		(US$)15.0%	% Per Sale

This network serves a wide variety of advertiser niches, so you'll need to evaluate their services and payouts to see if it's a good choice for you.

DirectLeads.com

DirectLeads is a Digital River company. If you've ordered software on the Internet, you've probably been billed through Digital River in many cases. Here are some of the verticals they serve:

- Retail
- Diet and Health
- Finance, Loans, Debt, Credit Card
- Entertainment
- Travel and Leisure
- Lead Brokers and Lead Generation
- Mobile, Broadband, Telephony, Internet
- Ringtones
- Software
- Dating
- Education
- Survey
- Service Industry

Performanced-Based.com

This is a "green" niche affiliate network with a long list of environmentally friendly and green companies for advertisers. Examples include:

Eco Nuts affiliate program: What are Soap Nuts™ : Eco Nuts™ Soap Nuts are a berry that grows in the Himalayas that naturally produces a soap. The soap is called saponin, a natural cleaner. Coming Soon!

Green Geeks affiliate program: Green Web Hosting: The World's #1 Green Energy Hosting Plan. Coming Soon!

Changers affiliate program: Changers Debuts World's First Social Energy.an intelligent personal solar charging kit that captures energy, records how much power it has generated, and then uploads precise metrics to the energy marketplace.

From Affiliatetips.com

Affiliatetips.com is a site that lists hundreds of affiliates by niche. Of course, each individual affiliate's products and services, as well as their payment amounts and procedures, must be checked out. However, if you're starting a website, blog, or social media page with a niche topic, here's one fast way to find the advertisers this site considers some of the best by niche. Let's look at some of them with screen shots from Affiliatetips. com based on their categorization of the advertisers by product or service niche.

Health Industry

THE BEST HEALTH AFFILIATE PROGRAMS

			QUICK FACTS	
myRXcash	**MYRXCASH DESCRIPTION** Top health affiliate network with high conversions. www.myrxcash.com VISIT SITE >		Base Commission: Commission type:	35% CPO
MarketHealth.com Health & Beauty Affiliate Network	**MARKET HEALTH DESCRIPTION** Leading affiliate network in a lucrative industry. Initial 50 % per sale commission. 1000s of Affiliate, 100s of Merchants! www.markethealth.com VISIT SITE >		Base Commission: Commission type:	$20 CPA
4Rx.com	**4RX.COM DESCRIPTION** Promote the new hyped and popular wonder pill, Rimonabant. 4RX.com is the only online pahrmacy that sells them! www.4rx.com/affiliate-program.html VISIT SITE >		Base Commission: Commission type:	25% CPO
MedStore Prescriptions and Health	**MEDSTORE DESCRIPTION** MedStore is a top-notch health affiliate program. Read more about what they have to offer. www.medstore.biz VISIT SITE >		Base Commission: Commission type:	29% CPO
AffiliatePharmacy Network.com	**AFFILIATEPHARMACYNETWORK.COM DESCRIPTION** Get 22 % CPO on pharmaceutical drugs, set your own product price and become a pharmaceutical reseller. www.affiliatepharmacynetwork.com VISIT SITE >		Base Commission: Commission type:	22% CPO
generic 4 all.com	**GENERIC4ALL DESCRIPTION** Join Generic4All in this healthy affiliate segment. Read more about it here. www.generic4all.com/ VISIT SITE >		Base Commission: Commission type:	30% CPO
AllergyStore.com	**ALLERGYSTORE.COM DESCRIPTION** Health affiliate program aimed at solving allergies. www.allergystore.com VISIT SITE >		Base Commission: Commission type:	10% CPO

The business of health is huge in this country, particularly with an aging population and baby-boomers hitting their retirement years. Throughout this book, I've mentioned fitness and health products because they are a great resource for affiliate income marketing.

You'll need a website or blog or some social media presence with on-topic discussions about health and health products, and then these links will fall right in for great income generation.

Mortgages

THE BEST MORTGAGE LOAN AFFILIATE PROGRAMS

	LOWERMYBILLS.COM DESCRIPTION	QUICK FACTS	
LowerMyBills.com	LowerMyBills.com provides a world wide service that helps consumers to lower their monthly bills. The company is mainly working with mortgages and other loans, but also with insurance, phone bills and similar areas. LowerMyBills has an ambitious affiliate program and pays well for each lead. www.lowermybills.com	Base Commission:	$70
		Commission type:	CPA
		VISIT SITE >	
Quicken Loans The Easiest Way to Get a Home Loan	QUICKENLOANS.COM DESCRIPTION Quicken Loans is one of the biggest and most trustworthy online mortgage lenders in the U.S. They help their clients with home loans, home equity loans and refinance loans. They have more than 4,000 mortgage experts ready to help your visitors and their conversion rate is good due to high-converting landing pages. www.quickenloans.com	QUICK FACTS Base Commission: Commission type: VISIT SITE >	$15 CPA
LendingTree	LENDINGTREE.COM DESCRIPTION LendingTree is one of the largest online lending exchanges in the U.S. It is a market place connecting visitors with multiple lenders that compete for their business. The LendingTree mortgage affiliate program pays you good money for each lead you generate. You receive up to $75 for each signup. www.lendingtree.com	QUICK FACTS Base Commission: Commission type: VISIT SITE >	$75 CPA

While the real estate industry has been taking a beating since 2008, it will be coming back. However, it's more difficult these days to get a mortgage, so online research is becoming a very popular tool for home buyers.

Marketing these type of affiliate links can be done in a number of ways and on a great many sites. I've even seen one affiliate who offered to write blog posts for lazy Realtors if she could place a link in the posts. They readily agreed because they wanted the free content. The links are then read by real estate shoppers, a very focused marketing approach. Or she just comments on their blogs and websites and adds links in the comments.

Online Casinos

THE BEST CASINO AFFILIATE PROGRAMS

		QUICK FACTS	
CASINOROOM.COM	**CASINOROOM DESCRIPTION** Get an exclusive deal through AffiliateTips.com at the CasinoRoom affiliate program. www.CasinoRoom.com	Base Commission: Commission type: VISIT SITE >	$175 CPA
Victor Chandler	**VICTOR CHANDLER DESCRIPTION** Victor Chandler - VC Affiliates offers you a great affiliate program with exceptional support. www.victorsaffiliates.com	Base Commission: Commission type: VISIT SITE >	$160 CPA
GLOBAL LIVE CASINO SEE YOUR CARDS DEALT	**GLOBAL LIVE CASINO DESCRIPTION** GlobalLiveCasino takes online gaming one step further than the competition. This unique casino brings you popular games broadcasted live from one of the most popular land based casinos in Europe, the Fitzwilliam Card Club & Casino www.globallivecasino.com	Base Commission: Commission type: VISIT SITE >	35% CPO
888.com CASINO	**888 CASINO DESCRIPTION** The online casino segment is hotter than ever. Great commission for you and big sign-up bonus for your referant! www.888.com	Base Commission: Commission type: VISIT SITE >	20% CPO
EURO PARTNERS	**EUROPARTNERS DESCRIPTION** Optimal clientele of online casino and poker brands! www.europartners.com	Base Commission: Commission type: VISIT SITE >	$75 CPA
betboo.com	**BETBOO DESCRIPTION** Betboo.com is the rising star of online gaming. www.Betboo.com	Base Commission: Commission type: VISIT SITE >	50% CPO

Gambling isn't going away, as human beings love the excitement and the infrequent winning day usually keeps them around even when they're losing more frequently.

Marketing for online casinos can be a great niche, especially if you're participating in gambling discussions or you've created a website or blog on the subject.

Dating Sites

THE BEST DATING AFFILIATE PROGRAMS

	Description	Quick Facts	
EasyDate Ltd Online Dating Solutions	**EASYDATE DESCRIPTION** Partner up with a highly converting dating affiliate program. www.easydate.biz VISIT SITE >	Base Commission: Commission type:	$80 CPA
easyflirt	**EASYFLIRT DESCRIPTION** EasyFlirt is a top dating affiliate program that has customers all over the world. www.easyflirt-partners.biz VISIT SITE >	Base Commission: Commission type:	55% CPO
FriendFinder.com	**FRIENDFINDER DESCRIPTION** This is an affiliate program that really has covered every possible angle in the dating segment. Big player with generous commissions. www.friendfinderinc.com/ VISIT SITE >	Base Commission: Commission type:	$50 CPA
chemistry	**CHEMISTRY DESCRIPTION** Backed up by the online dating site Match.com, Chemistry.com offer the best services and commissions! www.chemistry.com VISIT SITE >	Base Commission: Commission type:	$89 CPA
lavalife Where singles click.	**LAVALIFE DESCRIPTION** Being a dating affiliate is never boring. It's a fun and lively niche, and money-spinning to that. With the incredible 100% commission, all your marketing efforts go right back into your own pocket. To top it all, Lavalife runs a very consistent affiliate program. www.lavalife.com VISIT SITE >	Base Commission: Commission type:	$56 CPA
AmericanSingles	**AMERICAN SINGLES DESCRIPTION** 10 million members on a 400 million dollar market. Online dating is the latest in affiliate marketing! www.americansingles.com VISIT SITE >	Base Commission: Commission type:	$56 CPA

It would be very difficult to find a more profitable affiliate marketing niche than on dating and dating sites. This is especially true when you can target social media ads at single individuals. In the Facebook Ads discussion later, I'll show you just how targeted you can get.

The website PsychCentral.com disputed the theory that only lonely recluse-types use Internet dating sites with this statement:

The researchers found that people who are more "sociable are more likely to use Internet dating services than are those who are less sociable. This finding challenges the stereotypical profiling of Internet daters as being just lonely and socially anxious people."

Beauty Products

THE BEST BEAUTY AFFILIATE PROGRAMS

THE BODY SHOP	**THE BODY SHOP DESCRIPTION** The Body Shop is an internationally renowned brand and you now have the opportunity to earn money in promoting it on your website. www.thebodyshop.com	**QUICK FACTS** Base Commission: Commission type: VISIT SITE >	8% CPO
BUYME BEAUTY.com COSMETICS FOR LESS	**BUYMEBEAUTY.COM DESCRIPTION** The BuyMeBeauty.com affiliate program offers you the opportunity to make a fine income within a popular online niche - beauty. www.buymebeauty.com	**QUICK FACTS** Base Commission: Commission type: VISIT SITE >	12% CPO
g	**GREATSKIN.COM DESCRIPTION** GreatSkin.com affiliate program has a loyalty program in which sales totals accumulate instead of resetting to zero each month, earning you more money. www.greatskin.com	**QUICK FACTS** Base Commission: Commission type: VISIT SITE >	18% CPO
LAMAS BEAUTY	**LAMAS BEAUTY DESCRIPTION** Lamas Beauty has received several awards for its products, which are regularly featured in magazines as People and In-Style. www.lamasbeauty.com	**QUICK FACTS** Base Commission: Commission type: VISIT SITE >	27% CPO

A logical addition to your affiliate marketing of dating sites would be beauty products to help your advertisers' customers look their very best when they're taking that dating site photo. Also, the statement that Internet dating site users are actually very social by nature means that you should find a fertile marketing environment in the social media.

THE BEST EDUCATION AFFILIATE PROGRAMS

College and University.net	**COLLEGEANDUNIVERSITY DESCRIPTION** CollegeAndUniversity.net is one of the fastest growing online marketplaces for degree programs. www.collegeanduniversity.net	**QUICK FACTS** Base Commission: Commission type: VISIT SITE >	$30 CPA
PETERSON'S EssayEdge	**ESSAYEDGE DESCRIPTION** Big creative library; banners, text links, content linking or customized ads! www.essayedge.com	**QUICK FACTS** Base Commission: Commission type: VISIT SITE >	15% CPO
i-to-i TEFL Live. Travel. Earn!	**ONLINE TEFL COURSES DESCRIPTION** One of Online TEFL's top affiliates earned over £2000 in just 1 month! www.onlinetefl.com	**QUICK FACTS** Base Commission: Commission type: VISIT SITE >	10% CPO
Admissions Essays	**ADMISSIONSESSAYS DESCRIPTION** Admission Essays offers one of the best values on online academic application assistance. www.admissionsessays.com	**QUICK FACTS** Base Commission: Commission type: VISIT SITE >	$5 CPA
Language Course.net	**LANGUAGECOURSE DESCRIPTION** Recommended by the European Commission, you'll earn $20 for every enrollment! www.languagecourse.net	**QUICK FACTS** Base Commission: Commission type: VISIT SITE >	$30 CPA
Transparent Language	**TRANSPARENT LANGUAGE DESCRIPTION** There are many online language courses affiliate programs but this one differentiates itself from the others by providing	**QUICK FACTS** Base Commission: Commission type:	20% CPO

Education

Have you checked out the cost of a college degree at even a mediocre school lately? Parents start early trying to figure out how to fund it and how to choose a school that won't bankrupt them but will keep them in their children's good graces. Many education affiliate programs will be for college alternatives as well. There are also programs for services to college students.

Just Plain Shopping

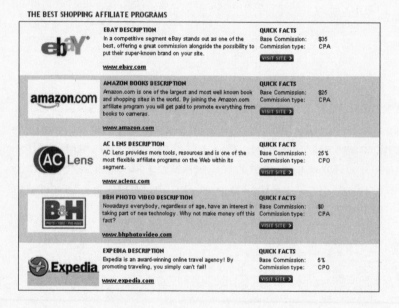

While a great many consumer products, particularly electronics, do not command high percentage affiliate commissions, they are in fact purchased so often that they can be very profitable for you.

Many affiliate marketers do quite well when they realize that Amazon.com is a huge marketplace where much more than books are sold. Amazon's stores sell just about anything you want, and their great service and shipping as well as their Amazon Prime membership benefits make them a repeat shopping destination.

Software

When it comes to software, people are buying millions of programs online every single day. People who work and play on computers also like to buy software that makes their work easier or their play more fun.

Software has great markups, much like I discussed in the information products chapter. These markups mean a lot more money available for affiliate marketing commissions, and software is a great niche for many affiliates.

You're getting the picture now. There are so many profitable niche markets for affiliate marketing. You can take a broad approach, a niche approach, or, like many, combine the two.

However, when you're using websites, blogs, and social media pages to market products, you will generally be focusing on a topic, and that's a niche market you'll want to target.

CHAPTER 8
Skimlinks and Viglinks

Everything I've told you about so far, and a lot of what we're going to talk about in future chapters about specific affiliate marketing platforms like social media and blogs, is about placing links to products, services, and vendors for affiliate commissions.

This chapter is a little different, because I'm talking about links placed automatically for you on your blogs, websites, and self-hosted forums. Two services, Skimlinks and Viglinks, provide this functionality. They both take a small commission off the top to deliver this service, which may not be something that interests you.

The reader who finds this information interesting is one who writes a lot of their own content on their own websites and blogs, or someone who hosts a forum or community website. If you want to learn about these services that automatically create links based on the text you enter into your blog posts and articles, this is the chapter to read. Instead of setting up affiliate accounts with a large group of vendor/advertisers, you simply write your content with advertiser names or regular links to their website products pages, and these services convert those links or words to an affiliate link that gets you paid. Let's see how it works.

Skimlinks

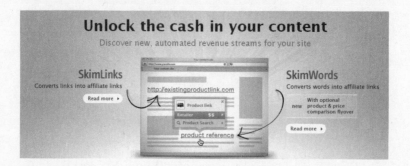

Skimlinks is primarily for content producers and bloggers. That's because the service takes your existing content and creates affiliate links for you without you having to set up individual affiliate accounts with advertisers. In fact, you'll get paid when links are sent to advertisers you didn't even know were part of the network.

Skimlinks says that they work with more than 17,000 merchants and that they can negotiate better affiliate commissions because the service sets up more links than the normal affiliate would be able to place. Because of the way the system works, links are set based on what you write, and the system also converts normal links. This means that affiliate marketers spend far less time researching a custom affiliate link and placing it. Most of that is done for them.

Phone Conversation: I just had a phone conversation with Support at Skimlinks and was given an example of their negotiation power and the fact that their fee in many cases will not cut your commission and can actually increase it. Amazon.com was the example, and I learned that Skimlinks has negotiated a 25% to 50% better commission for their affiliates than they get with a direct affiliation with Amazon.

While Skimlinks takes 25% of the commission off the top for the service, their claim is that the better commissions they negotiate, plus the many more links the affiliate will have through this automated process, will more than make up for their service commission cost.

Blogs & Editorial

From niche blogs to editorial sites – if you have an engaged audience and good traffic, you could be earning through Skimlinks.

Forums & Communities

If your forum or community loves to discuss products and services, Skimlinks could unlock a new revenue stream you'd usually miss.

News Sites

When monetizing your news site, you'll need a flexible solution to suit your sensitive content – Skimlinks could be the answer.

Acceptance is on a site-by-site basis, and not everyone gets approved. Here's what Skimlinks says:

We have a strict approval process because we want quality publishers in our network that add value to our merchants and the entire affiliate ecosystem!

When a publisher applies, we vet each site and only approve those that meet our standards and qualify under merchant terms. Because we hold the power of aggregating so many mer-

chants, we have to be responsible with who we allow to use our service, so we only approve sites that merchants would approve themselves.

But when it's this good, it's worth working for - get approved once for Skimlinks, and you'll be able to start earning immediately from 17,000+ merchants. Imagine trying to get approved on all those on your own!

If you have a quality blog, website, or online forum, you'll likely get approved. There are bits of code that must be placed into the site to allow Skimlinks to work, which is why you must own the site. This won't work in the social media or comments you place on other people's sites.

Here's what Skimlinks says may get your site turned down:
- Lack of content
- Sensitive content (certain types of 'adult' content, for example)
- Content that is likely unsuitable for affiliate marketing (like political or religious content)
- Content with minimal opportunities for automated affiliate marketing (e.g. not focused on products and services available to buy online)
- Websites with audiences in locations that are outside our coverage

However, there are probably readers of this book who are already active in creating content on their own sites and blogs that will be great for affiliate product marketing, and Skimlinks can have you up and running in minutes; they can even convert text and links in what you've already published.

Why would you bother to use Skimlinks and let them have a piece of the commission, even if a small one? This chapter will be of interest to people who are blogging or have sites they own with a lot of content that relates well to products, such as travel-related sites, photography sites, fashion, health and fitness, or just about any other topic or niche with related products and services.

Even if you're not already blogging, if you decide that setting up niche blogs or mini-sites to write about topics and place affiliate links is the way you want to go, then you may choose to use Skimlinks because it can result in many more links with less time and effort on your part.

Keep in mind that once you set up a blog or site to use Skimlinks, that's one site strategy, but they do not have a problem with you placing other direct affiliate links on your site, as well. You can continue to promote any affiliates or merchants outside of Skimlinks that you want. Let's talk about the two ways links are set by Skimlinks. They are Skimlinks and Skimwords.

Skimlinks
Instead of going to your Commission Junction or other affiliate network account and getting a specific product link to recommend let's say the Canon Powershot camera line, you would just place a link to that line's page at the Canon Website and Skimlinks would convert the link to a Skimlink affiliate link.

Instead of having to set up an affiliate account with each camera manufacturer, or with large retailers who sell those cameras, we're working with Skimlinks on our photography blog for this example. So I'm writing a post about the Canon Powershot line of cameras, and I want to link to that line's main page at the Canon site. Canon is one of the merchants working with Skimlinks, so this is what I do:

http://shop.usa.canon.com/webapp/wcs/stores/servlet/subCategory_10051_10051_-1_17757

That's the link I use in my post, usually as a text link such as <u>see the Canon Powershot line here</u>.

However, once Skimlinks sees a link to an affiliate site, it is converted, and this one ended up looking like this:

http://go.redirectingat.com/?id=16402X734245&site=gaxxxxxx xx.com&xs=1&url=http%3A%2F%2Fshop.usa.canon.com%2Fwe bapp%2Fwcs%2Fstores%2Fservlet%2FsubCategory_10051_1005 1_-1_17757&xguid=5ce883747cb7650aae93d6d0da24e934&xcre o=0&sref=http%3A%2F%2Fgalleryrealtyoftaos.com%2F%3Fp% 3D44490%26preview%3Dtrue

Notice that my link has been redirected to create an affiliate link to make sure I get paid. I didn't have to go find an affiliate link, nor create one for that specific page at the Canon camera website, since Skimlinks takes care of that.

Here is the merchant record at Skimlinks for Canon, and it shows some average statistics. The average basket size is over $200.00, but the conversion rate is only 0.71%. This is important when we get to the section below this one about Skimwords.

Before that, though, let's talk about the low conversion rate for Canon's direct site affiliate links. Of course, the manufacturer's site is where we'll normally pay MSRP, the retail price. So even if someone were to follow that link, we probably won't get paid because they'll just go shopping around the Web for a better price, as most of us do.

Now, I could take the approach of helping my readers by linking them both to the Canon Powershot page for details and specifications, then placing a second link like "get a better price at Target." Target is also a Skimlinks merchant, and their conversion rate is higher than Canon's. Here's the link I would place to the Target page of Powershot Cameras:

http://www.target.com/s?searchTerm=canon+powershot&categ ory=0%7CAll%7Cmatchallany%7Call+categories

However, here's what Skimlinks does with it:

http://www.target.com/s?searchTerm=canon+powershot&categ ory=0%7CAll%7Cmatchallany%7Call+categories&ref=tgt_adv_ xasd0001&AFID=Performics_Skimlinks&LNM=Primary

So I can choose vendors rather than just go with the manufacturer's site. I can even make it a positive customer relations move by recommending a lower-priced resource.

Now let's say you're a writer on a mission, and you want to write, write a lot, and mention a lot of products without having to go chase down links. This is where Skimwords comes into play.

Skimwords
Skimwords recognizes brand and product names and will automatically convert them to affiliate links. Now you're not involved in the selection of the page where the consumer ends up, but Skimwords is supposed to be looking out for you by choosing a page and merchant with good conversion numbers. This is logical, since their commission depends on conversions just like yours does.

So in my photography blog post about Canon Powershot cameras, I instead use the words "Canon Powershot." That's what

I type right into a sentence, and I don't even think about going and getting a link. Here's what Skimwords does with it:

1. It highlights and makes those words a link…Canon Powershot

2. That link is an affiliate link assigned by Skimwords. In this case: http://www.ebay.com/itm/NEW-Canon-PowerShot-SX230-HS-12-1-MP-Digital-Camera-Black-/270867364156?afsrc=1#ht_500wt_1156

3. That link has my affiliate code and takes the consumer to a place to learn about and purchase a Canon Powershot camera. The next image shows that page in this example. Now is it the best place? Skimwords must think so, but you can use the previous approach and take more time in choosing your own destination/ landing page.

However, the real advantage here is for the writer who wants to create a whole lot of content mentioning a many brands and products and have Skimwords do the work of locating a landing page for purchase and setting the link. Here's that page:

It turns out to be a top-rated eBay store page, as eBay is also set up with Skimwords.

The Writing Advantage

If you're going about your days writing product reviews or taking content (legal and approved) from manufacturer or other sites and placing it on a blog, a website, or in a forum you operate, then Skimwords can make it faster, easier, and more profitable for you.

You're just cranking out the content and using the right brand names and product words, and Skimwords is doing the rest. If you already have a blog with a lot of text, you may have money waiting just by setting it up with Skimlinks and installing the code on the site. All of those words you already created will suddenly become affiliate links for commissions.

Profit Secret Even Skimlinks Hasn't Mentioned

I'm going to give you here a secret that I just discovered by testing, and I can't find any mention of this strategy anywhere, including on the Skimlinks site.

Skimlinks only works on sites or blogs you own, so you'll still have to create those sites and blogs to get them approved and get the code installed. You'll need to write some great content and link out to the products and manufacturers. Using our previous example, you'll still need that photography blog, which you may already have. Or it could be a diet, fitness, fashion, etc. blog or site.

You CAN use social media!

I've stated in this chapter that you can't use Skimlinks on your Facebook or Google+ pages, and that's the truth. You don't own those sites, and the code can't be installed. However, many affiliate marketers are doing the bulk of their product and affiliate writing on social media sites.

I did a test, and I'll let you see the results. I didn't try it on Face-book, but it should work the same as it did on Google+, and I did it with a WordPress blog, though there are other ways and other blogging platforms.

I went to a Google+ business page and wrote a test post with the words Canon Powershot in it. I wanted to see if there was a way to get that post into my blog with Skimlinks able to con-vert the words with Skimwords into an affiliate link.

With WordPress you use a "plugin" to install the Skimlinks code. With other sites, the HTML or Java code is given to you to paste into the appropriate place on your site. That's how Skim-links is able to do its job. There's another plugin for WordPress that I'll tell you more about later, but it's one that takes your Google+ posts and places them into your blog if they're public at Google+. So I went over to one of my Google+ pages and wrote this post:

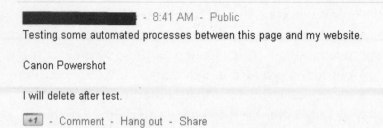

- 8:41 AM - Public

Testing some automated processes between this page and my website.

Canon Powershot

I will delete after test.

+1 - Comment - Hang out - Share

Notice that I just typed in Canon Powershot, without doing any-thing to link it out. Once it had time to be picked up by that plugin, the post appeared on the site this way:

Canon Powershot

I will delet Shopping link added by SkimWords

Google+: View post on Google+

Post imported by Google+Blog. Created By Daniel Treadwell.

I hovered over the linked Canon Powershot text to produce that box with the information that the link was added by Skim-words.

So I can build a bunch of niche-oriented pages over in Google+, do most of my writing over there, and they'll move over to my niche blogs, and Skimwords will create the links for income. I have the choice of whether to place actual links to be converted and redirected or to rely on Skimwords catching the product and brand text and doing the linking for me. Actually, a combination is the best approach. Place links in your text and use product and brand references.

RSS Feed Strategy

Though I used a plugin and a WordPress blog, you should be able to use RSS feeds from your Facebook account or even create them for Google+ pages to get the text of posts in those media to move into your blogs or websites automatically. Use of RSS is a common practice for displaying other sites' content in your sites or blogs. Whether Skimwords converts the text may depend on the feed, so you'll have to test.

I'll give you some information on getting the RSS feed for a Facebook page in a later chapter. I'll also give you a way to create an RSS feed for a Google+ page in the chapter on using

Google+ for affiliate marketing. Google+ at the time I'm writing this doesn't provide RSS feeds for pages, so you'll need to use this trick to create your own.

The Best of Both Worlds

Another discussion on my phone call to Skimlinks Support centered on other links in posts that pass from Google+ or come in from an RSS feed or other cross-posting service. Skimlinks will recognize other service affiliate links and leave them alone, but they will convert and redirect other non-affiliate links.

So you can now write a post in Google+ on your photography-oriented niche business page. You can use product and brand names and let Skimwords catch and convert them. Or you can enter a link to the manufacturer or merchant page where you want the visitor to end up, and Skimlinks will convert and redirect it. OR you can enter a specific affiliate link from another network or your direct relationship with an advertiser, and Skimlinks will ignore it, leaving it to direct the visitor to a page that pays you through another affiliate agreement.

Now you can write your Google+ or Facebook content and have it work for you at the social media site, and work for you again at the blog or website where it's being cross-posted. Write it once and use it multiple times!

If you're not into trying to write a lot of content to get a blog approved by Skimlinks right away, set up the blog anyway. Use feeds and cross-posting to write a lot in the social media and have it cross-posted to your niche blog. As it builds out, at some point you should end up with enough content that you can get it accepted by Skimlinks. Once it is, installing the code will get any Skimwords brand and product references in past content converted immediately.

That's the basic scoop on Skimlinks and Skimwords, so let's look
at a competitor.

VigLinks

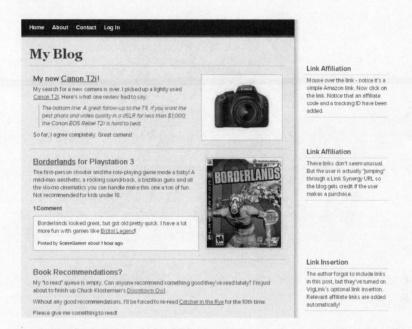

I won't go into detail, as the services of VigLink are very similar
to those of Skimlinks. Take a look at both services and make a
decision.

If you're not sitting on a lot of content, you may want to table
this decision for awhile. You may find that once you start building out content with cross-posting, using one of these services
will make a lot of sense since it doubles your exposure for the
same content and provides a way to use one post to promote
different affiliates in multiple places.

CHAPTER 9
Websites for Affiliate Marketing

Affiliate marketers use websites as one marketing tool when they're promoting affiliate links on niche topics. Every type of product or service we've discussed so far in this book would be a candidate for a custom website just to write content about it and place affiliate links and image ads.

The image above shows the various considerations the website owner has when getting the site up and running. It can intimidate the beginner, but that needn't be the case. Website hosting and design providers have come a long way, and all of these considerations are handled for you by the online service and at very low cost. There is no reason why you can't have multiple websites for a very low monthly cost, each serving a different niche market.

You can search on the Web for "easy website design," like I did, and find hundreds of candidates. In this chapter I'm going to give you some examples that work and are inexpensive, but feel free to do your own investigation. The last example will be a Community Network Forum type of site, which has a somewhat different objective than the others.

Weebly

Weebly is a popular website solution that provides everything you need to build out a website and promote it on the Internet. Hosting, which I'll talk about again in relation to blogging, is simply the selling of "space" on the Web where your site resides. Your site must sit on a Web server somewhere, and space is what you're paying for. What you put in that space is your business. However, all of the services I'm going to tell you about in this chapter provide hosting for your site as a part of the package.

The other site location service is your Domain Name. The domain name is separate from the hosted space, but a domain name registrar can also be your hosting service. The services we're talking about in this chapter will assign a domain name, normally some type of sub-domain of the service domain, and they'll also allow you to purchase a custom domain name like YourSite.com.

So you have a website sitting somewhere on a server, and you pay a registrar to reserve and let you use a domain name to take people to that server location to find your site. Again, things are simple, as you'll get all of this with the services I'm telling you about.

Back to Weebly specifically.

Drag & Drop Website Builder

Weebly offers a simple template design drag-n-drop interface. The image shows how the user drags elements of the page around to place them where desired. Boxes can be moved, text entered into the boxes, and images placed by uploading them.

| Drag & Drop Website Builder |
| 100+ Professional Themes |
| Powerful Hosting |
| Fast & Helpful Support |
| Easy Blogging |
| Photo Galleries & Slideshows |
| Video & Audio Players |
| Easy Form Builder |
| ImagePerfect Image Editor |
| Detailed Traffic Stats |
| Free Domain Hosting |
| No Forced Advertising |
| More Features... |

In addition to the drag & drop interface, Weebly offers a large number of themes. These are templates with layout selections and color schemes.

Blogging is also a feature allowed with Weebly, so if you plan on blogging as well, this is a way to do both with one service. Before you decide, read the blogging chapter and learn how you can use WordPress blogging software as a complete website tool. There are powerful tools available doing it that way that may not be available using these template services.

Weebly also has video and audio players to showcase your video and audio content if you use it in your promotions. The next few items are going to be features of many of these website services, so we'll talk about them once here, and then just mention them later as needed.

Website Forms

One of the tabs in the image, Easy Form Builder, is about adding website forms to collect visitor contact information. Especially if you're email marketing, you'll want to use forms and special offers of information, free trials, or product samples to get visitors to give up their email address so that you can follow up with marketing. I'm going to go into this in detail in a future chapter.

Image Editing

Another Weebly feature is a built-in image editor so that you can resize images, as well as improve their quality through simple adjustments to brightness, contrast, and other photo characteristics.

Traffic Statistics

Also called "Analytics," Weebly and most other services will have some type of statistical site traffic reporting. You'll want to know where visitors came from, what pages they landed on, how many pages they visited, and where they moved around your site. You use these stats to learn what draws visitors and which pages are selling for you.

SEO, Search Engine Optimization

Weebly and the other services do a certain amount of optimization of your site to help you get better search engine positioning. However, only so much can be done with sitemaps and other strategies. In the end, it all boils down to your content, which must be relevant to your niche and must be original. The more relevant and original content you publish, the better your chances of getting to the first page of search results.

One of the reasons for blogging is that it gets you into the habit of publishing new content on a regular basis. This is one thing search engines value, and having a blogging function in Weebly is a plus.

eCommerce

If you decide you want to offer products or services of your own, Weebly provides an eCommerce function that lets you upload product images, place descriptions, and price them in a store application. This isn't the goal of affiliate marketing, but I wanted to touch on it as an offered feature.

Mobile-Optimized Sites

An important feature is the automated creation of mobile optimized sites. People are moving to the mobile Internet in a huge way. Weebly creates a mobile version of the site that recognizes a mobile device visit and presents the site appropriately for display on smaller screens.

Password-Protected Pages

One option that is used by some affiliate marketers in order to capture visitors is special access to information on protected pages. By password-protecting a page, you can offer a mail link or a form on your site offering the password via email. By doing this, you have their email address for follow-up marketing.

Weebly Wrap-up

Weebly is popular because it's either free or inexpensive. Adding features can cost around $5/month, which is an inexpensive solution for incorporating all of these features into one web platform that's easy to use.

Intuit

Intuit is well-known for its QuickBooks accounting product. Now they also offer an online service for hosting and building websites for small business.

I'm not going to go into lengthy explanations of features again, as I've gone over that with Weebly. For these other sites, just compare features, decide what you need to build your site and market with it, and go from there. You may need only the most basic of site plans.

The Mini-Site
Many affiliate marketers build out a very simple and basic website, don't blog, but just put up pages of information about their niche, and then post affiliate links. This can be effective, and it takes no maintenance time once it's set up. If this is your approach, you may be able to use a very basic and inexpensive template system. Here's the Intuit plan selection chart with prices:

Starter	Business	Business Plus
$7.99/Mo	$19.99/Mo	$49.99/Mo
Get a basic website	Get a professional site with a custom domain	Everything you need to grow your business.
Try It Free	Try It Free	Try It Free
5 Pages	100 Pages	Unlimited Pages
25MB Storage	5GB Storage	10GB Storage
Online tools & Phone support	Online tools & Phone support	Online tools & Phone support
Hundreds of customizable templates	Hundreds of customizable templates	Hundreds of customizable templates
Site statistics	Site statistics	Site statistics
	1 Domain	3 Domains
	5 Email boxes	50 Email boxes
		Business Listings
		Search Engine Marketing
		Available add-ons:
		Traffic Booster
		Sell Online

A mini-site would probably be just fine on the $7.99 plan. However, go back and compare it to Weebly feature-by-feature, as the free Weebly platform may offer more at no ongoing cost.

Hostgator & Soholaunch

For the simplest approach, one of the two platforms we just discussed is probably best. However, for flexibility and the ability to expand, I'm going to give you a somewhat different approach now. It's setting up a hosting account of your own that allows you to build multiple websites or blogs and have multiple domain names. A popular resource for this approach is Hostgator.com.

The image shows the basic Hostgator account prices, which you'll find very reasonable, especially considering that they offer toll free phone support in America. The Baby Plan offers unlimited domains, disk space, and bandwidth for visitors and downloads.

The approach we're going to take here is to host with a Baby Plan and do what we want with it. In the blogging chapter, I'll mention Hostgator again as the service you can use to host multiple WordPress blogs, as well. If we're sticking with websites, you can use this plan and a free application in Hostgator to build multiple websites with an application called Soholaunch. First I should mention the free website design templates offered as a service of the Hostgator account, since there are many based on business types:

However, for more flexibility and features, there are free and paid versions of Soholaunch. With many more templates and functions available, it's something to consider.

Here's the basic chart of functions for Soholaunch:

The Community Forum Site With Ning.com

YOUR KEY TO AN AWESOME SOCIAL COMMUNITY

Create a perfect social website to bring people together. With your own look and feel, and choice of social integration, Ning opens new doors to revenue and involvement.

LEARN MORE

There is another completely different approach to marketing to a niche audience. And the more passionate people are about a niche, the more likely that this type of site can work for the affiliate marketer. I'm using Ning.com as the example, since it's the largest, and it grew by catering to affiliate marketers.

What you're doing here is creating your own social network based on a community. That community can be a real geographical community, such as one for your city, but for affiliate marketers it's going to be a community of users interested in a single niche.

To use as an example here, I chose a network created for people who camp with VWs. That's a bit too small of a niche perhaps than you would need for your site, but the site uses most of the features available in Ning, so they're good for an example. The site is at http://vwcamperfamily.ning.com/ .

Because it's an example of what you can do with Ning, I didn't even try to check out links in posts and forums that could be affiliate links, but I know there are going to be some there, perhaps a huge number.

It really doesn't matter, since you place your affiliate advertising where you want it and as often as you desire. Also, this site isn't nearly as pretty as you can customize a Ning site to be, so ignore the design as a factor.

The purpose here is to show you how to use a more social network type of website to build a large group of enthusiastic users who contribute content so you don't have to write as much. Also, since we discussed Skimlinks and Skimwords previously, you should know that you can set it up on a Ning site, and every recognized product or brand word combination in your users' posts and discussions will automatically become affiliate links for income!

The image shows the home page of this Ning site, and you can see the tabs across the top showing that they are using the major functions of Ning that work for the site because they work for users. Once you join, it's like joining a mini-social network. However, this network is a group of people with an interest in the site's niche, in this case camping with VW vehicles.

Then there are various functions that you set up as the site administrator, allowing your users to upload content, including photos, videos, and even their own blog. Anyway, let's work through some of those tabbed functions to see how they work and how they can generate income for you.

Forum

In the forum, you have ongoing discussions about any topic that is started as a Discussion by your users. In the next image, we see some of the current discussions going on between members.

I noticed the one at the arrow at the bottom, as it specifically asks a question, which brings up a great affiliate marketing opportunity. You would only be doing a site like this if you were marketing for advertisers and manufacturers of camping equipment of interest to this niche. So you'll be able to get an affiliate link for both acrylic and canvas pop tops.

Let's say you go to this discussion and help this user by answering their question. You should try, for credibility reasons, to shed light on the comparison of the two top types, and if you don't know enough to do that, then go to the Web and find an article or a video you can link to that will help them decide. However, in the post, let them know that you have a couple of sources known for quality tops of both types, and give them links (affiliate of course!)

Many advertisers or manufacturers will have great instructional material on their site, and an affiliate link can take the prospect directly to it, setting a cookie on their hard drive. That way, as long as the cookie is live, you get paid no matter where on the site they go as long as they buy something.

Your goal over time with this type of site is to not be SELLING, instead be selling. You want to become respected as someone knowledgeable about the site niche and helpful in getting your users' questions answered and building discussions of interest to users. You'll be placing affiliate links, but in this helpful context, you won't be placing them everywhere there's free space on the page.

Groups
This tab is for segmentation of users into groups based on other common interests.

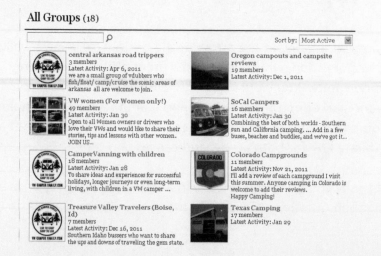

The Groups function allows your users to join groups with more focused interests. Here you can see that most of the groups are related to location. However, depending on your niche, it could be groups like Tent Camping, RV Camping, etc.

Each group has its own forum, so the group members can keep their discussions focused on their shared interest and group dynamics. So the VW women (For Women only!) forum would definitely be discussions of interest to women VW Camper members.

Events

The Events tab is very popular on sites where people have local gatherings or clubs. Your members can add their own group events with location details and even map them. Your site becomes more than just a place to talk about common interests; it becomes the place to go to keep up with what is happening.

Blogs

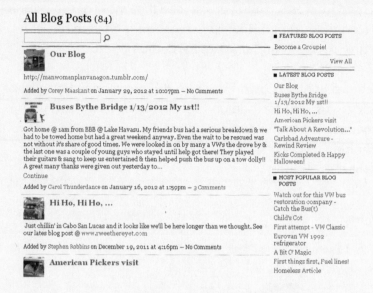

Offering blogs is optional, but you should do it for two reasons. First, you are offering a service to your members, as they can blog about this niche and their passion for it, and they don't have to go build a blog somewhere else.

However, of much more value to you is the content they're writing. Think about it. Get a few hundred people all blogging about your niche, and the keywords are building up dramatically on your site. Your search engine placement will benefit hugely from this content, and you don't have to write a word!

The Community Site's Benefits & Requirements

As you can see, there are some great benefits derived from taking this approach to a website. Instead of you doing all of the writing, or having a static website with little new content because you don't have time to write it, you have a whole group of people all happily building your content for you.

The group dynamic is great, and you know that every product and service affiliate link you have will be visible to people who are only there because of their interest in your niche. Your CTR, Click-Through-Ratio for links will be better than it would be in many other locations where you could place the same links. However, the time requirements are going to be a lot greater for you with this type of site. You'll need to constantly monitor it, write new material, engage with your members, answer questions, and more. So it's unlikely that you would consider this approach for more than one or two niche sites. And, they should be niche markets that are your passion, as well. That's the only way you'll do them justice.

At the time I'm writing this, the site you would build for effective affiliate marketing would probably be the service level that Ning charges out at $29.95/month. So cost is an issue, as well. And, remember that it's not going to be effective at all unless you can build up a very large membership.

At this time, I think you can probably do almost as well if you can get a Facebook and Google+ page going for your niche topics, and both of those are free. They're also about social connection and community. However, there are major benefits in the Ning approach for a large community site with many features for the members.

You have several excellent options now if your marketing plan includes websites. However, reserve a decision until you get through the next chapter on blogging for affiliate marketing. You'll be able to do everything you've seen in this chapter, build out multiple sites that don't have to look like blogs, and have a large number of sites out there for under $10/month total.

CHAPTER 10

Blogging as an Affiliate Marketer

We've learned about websites now, but it's important to consider blogging as a complete Web presence strategy. By Web
presence I mean what you're doing outside of the social networks, as in sites that you own and control. The previous website chapter shows that it isn't difficult or expensive to build one
or more websites for affiliate marketing. However, let's make
one thing clear about websites and blogs.

Blogging's Growth

Early on, when blogs first became popular, they all looked the
same. You know, those columns on the screen, a lot of text, not
much in the way of images, pretty boring actually. So if they
didn't look as good as what you could do with a website, why
blog anyway?

Blogs became popular in large part due to the simplicity of publishing content. People started personal blogs to speak their

mind on the Web, but to do it easily. Blogs were simple, and it was easy to post since they were a lot like using a word processor. That simplicity in the beginning was possible in part due to the limited feature set and formatting.

As it became clear that the ease of use increased the number of published posts and articles, it also became clear that the search engines loved blogs. This regular new content drew visits from the search engine robots more frequently, and the search engines gave additional priority to newer content.

Once businesses realized the advantages of blogging, they jumped in with both feet. As more businesses came on board with the various blogging platforms, the platforms began to add to their functionality and creative formatting. They've gotten better and better over time. I'm going to use WordPress for all of the blogging discussion, as WordPress is the most widely-used blogging platform, and it is the major player in the blogging world and now in the website world as a whole.

A Blog is a Website!

As WordPress updated its feature set and grew to be the big player, it also became clear that the line between what was called a "website" and what was called a "blog" was disappearing. The current version of WordPress allows the user to build out a website/blog, either, or a combination.

You can build the same look for static web pages and have the blog as a location on the site but not necessarily the home page.

So let's say this once with conviction: *A WordPress blog site can look and act like a website or a blog or both, and your visitor won't be able to tell the difference.* In fact, you would be very surprised to discover that a great many major websites you visit are actually built with free WordPress software. Here are a few notable WordPress users:

Everything you could do in the previous website chapter you can do with WordPress software, and that software is free of charge. All you have to do is have it installed in your own hosting account or use the free hosting provided by WordPress.com. There are major differences, so let's explain them so you can make the right decision.

Free Software & Hosting at WordPress.com

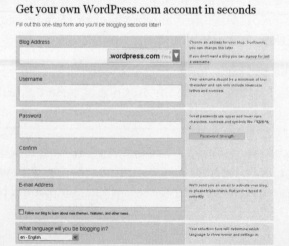

If you go to WordPress.com, you'll see the screen shot above, and in five minutes you can have a blog! Your address on the Web will be YourSiteName.wordpress.com, as you see in the first box. You can point a domain name from any registrar to this site, so you don't have to use the WordPress URL in your marketing.

Because you're taking the free hosting from WordPress.com, you will be significantly limited in what you can do and the features you can use for your site, especially those provided by third parties. I mentioned plugins in a previous chapter; you won't be able to use plugins if you go with the fully free strategy.

If your Web marketing strategy is to create many small sites, each focused on a niche, then the fully free WordPress strategy could be perfect for you. You can still do just about anything you want in the way of formatting. However, you'll be limited in the number of pre-designed themes from which you can choose. There are a couple hundred or more available with the free hosting, while there are tens of thousands you can install if you take the paid hosting route I'll explain next.

Creating many small, focused niche strategy sites can be a great use of the fully free strategy. They'll be effective and get your marketing out there, and you'll not spend a penny for the hosting, software, or Web exposure.

Self-Hosting WordPress

The difference with this approach is that you'll be paying to host your WordPress software. Using your own hosting service and their servers, you won't have the restrictions imposed by the free approach. Remember the Hostgator discussion in the previous chapter and that Hostgator will provide the account for hosting as many blogs as you want for under $10/month.

That Baby hosting account that I showed you previously allows unlimited blogs and bandwidth, so you can create one after another in the same account. Each is totally independent of the others, but you can then use plugins and choose from thousands of themes, some custom-designed for your specific purpose. Most themes are free; others cost a small amount for a lifetime license.

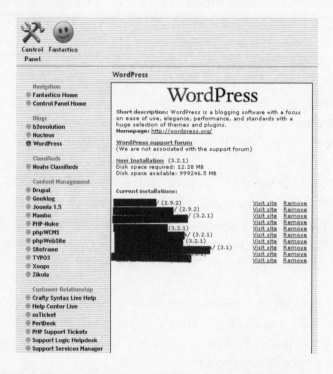

The image above shows the Fantastico application in Hostgator that allows a very fast 10 minute installation of the free WordPress software in the account. The blacked-out area is of eight blog sites this user has installed in this account, each one an independent site with its own domain name.

Once you've installed the software, the default theme for WordPress shows up as your site, and you can then go into the Dashboard and install your own themes and customize the site the way that you want it.

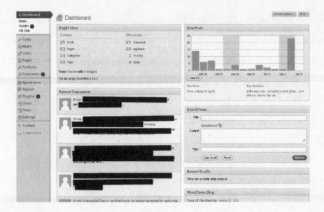

The image above is a shrunken version of the Dashboard for WordPress. The tabs on the left all expand into sub-selections, and you manage your entire site from the Dashboard. You can also select what you see on this screen and move the elements around.

I mentioned before that hosting your own WordPress installations frees up all of the power and third party functions, themes, and plugins for your use. There are even themes designed with affiliate marketers in mind. They make it easier to incorporate affiliate links, at least according to their designers. Here are a couple themes that turned up in a search:

Posting Articles in the Blog

I've previously told you that it's really easy to post into a Word-Press blog. I want to show you a screen shot of a post in the creation or edit phase in WordPress to let you see the tools available for you and to see how easy it is to enter text or to add images, audio, and video to your site.

The WordPress posting interface is a lot like a word processor or many other places where you've entered data or text on the Internet.

The image shows a post being edited/created, and you can see that there are a number of icons above the text. Those allow you to format text, note the Bold and Italic icons you are used to seeing, as well as use many other formatting options. There are also icons to insert an image, just like you would in a word processor.

You can buy a hundred "Dummies" type books that will get you up and running with WordPress very quickly, so I'm not going to go into more detail here. Just know that it's an easy blogging platform to use, and if you want simple sites, it's totally free.

Plugins for WordPress

I have mentioned plugins several times, and specifically the Skimlinks and Skimwords plugin that lets that service monetize your blog based on the links you place in it and the product and brand words you use in your posts, articles, and pages.

There are many plugins designed to provide special functionality for affiliate marketers. I did a search on "affiliate market" from the Add New Plugins section of the Dashboard, and here are a few of many results.

It's not just about affiliate marketing plugins, though. There are plugins to do just about anything you can imagine or desire on your site. There are podcasting, video, and audio plugins, and a great many more. Almost all are free.

Skimlinks Plugin
Most plugins, once installed, will have settings to adapt their performance and functionality to what you desire for your WordPress site. The Skimlinks settings page is simple:

Usually the default settings of a plugin are fine to start with until you learn how all of the settings work and why.

Federal law has been enacted to address blogging about products for compensation. Whether we agree about the necessity of such laws, they make it illegal in some cases to blog about products and get compensated unless we disclose the fact that we're compensated. Skimlinks has some HTML code to place a badge on your site to make that disclosure.

The image shows the creation of the badge, with selections as to appearance. Then just copy the HTML and paste it into the sidebar of your WordPress blog, normally at the bottom of all other content in that sidebar.

You're going to find a number of plugins that will make your site work better, display better, and convert affiliate links to income better, as well. So don't hesitate to search for plugins with keywords if you have an idea for enhancing your Word-Press site.

Now you know enough to make a decisions about blogging and the platform you want to use. In the next chapter we'll look at cross-posting between blogs or social media sites.

CHAPTER 11

Blog & Social Media Cross-Posting

I don't want to drive you over the edge with the possibilities here, but the goal is to write something once and use it more than once. This is efficient, and it gets your content into more than one place where it can generate income. Keep in mind that everyone has their preferences as to where they spend the most time online.

One person will spend most of their time on Facebook, another on Google+, still another using Twitter, and many will be reading their favorite blogs. Most people will use several of these online resources, but they'll always spend the most time on one of them. With that in mind, we want to have our content in as many places as possible, but we don't want to have to copy/paste or rewrite it.

Understanding RSS Feeds

I mention RSS feeds throughout this book, so let's be sure that you have a basic understanding of how they work again here, because they play a major role in our content multiple-use strategy. They also are a major part of blogging.

While some websites use RSS, almost all blogs do. It stands for Really Simple Syndication. Syndication is the placement of content on more than one site on the Web. Blogs are set up to create an RSS feed item, sort of like a mini-press release, for every post you write on the blog.

An RSS feed is the mechanism for getting the press release out to the world. However, it doesn't just shoot it out there like a shotgun. Let's look at the sequence of events that happens when you write a new post on a blog:

1. You write a post and hit the Publish button to make it live on your blog site.
2. An immediate RSS feed item is created.
3. Anyone who has "subscribed" to your RSS feed for that blog will receive that feed item in their Feed Reader.

An RSS feed is set up to either send out the entire content of a post along with the title or to send out an excerpt of the post. An excerpt requires that the recipient click the title and leave their feed reader to go to the blog and read the post. It's a preference thing, but the best way is usually to send the entire content. That way no other action is necessary on the part of the recipient to read all of your post and have access to the affiliate links right out of their feed reader.

Here's the issue though: *less than a quarter of all Internet users understand or even know about RSS and use feed readers.* If that's the case, why are we bothering to learn about them here? It's because they can be used "behind the scenes" to feed items to websites, other blogs, and the social media without any knowledge or involvement of the site visitor.

So a person reading the items on your Facebook Fan Page for your dietary supplement information will not know that this newest post came from somewhere else. You wrote it for your blog, and a Facebook App pulled in the feed and placed it into your Facebook Wall. You wrote it once and used it twice in this case.

However, that's in one direction, and I'm going to show you how to use RSS and WordPress Plugins to go in either direction you choose. In other words, you can take a post you write on your Facebook page, and it can be automatically displayed as a post on your blog.

Before we look at the ways to move information by "cross-posting," here's one more thing about RSS. An RSS feed item is created by a large piece of programming code, called XML. That's all you really need to know about the code, since you use a URL placed in appropriate places display your content. Here's an example of a Facebook outgoing RSS URL:

http://www.facebook.com/feeds/page.php?id=128499187312&format=rss20

If you click it directly, you'll see a page full of code. However, when it's placed into the proper place in a blog or social media recipient application, the code just runs and the RSS feed of the posts is displayed.

Gallery Realty of Taos - A Buyer Brokerage

The average depth to water and average well depths in the Taos real estate MLS 40+...
Taos Real Estate

The average depth to water and average well depths in the Taos real estate MLS 40+ areas is of great interest to buyers. This is a high desert area, and there is a concern on the part of buyers to understand the availability of water. Get the New Mexico State Engineer's Offi...
Published: 29 January 2012, 10:21 pm
More stories: Read more stories
Custom tabs: View example tabs
...
See More

Like · Comment · Share · January 30 at 7:48am via Social RSS

Gallery Realty of Taos - A Buyer Brokerage

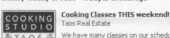

Cooking Classes THIS weekend!
Taos Real Estate

We have many classes on our schedule over the next several weeks - here are the ones in the near future including THIS weekend - hope you can join us! Call 575 776 2665 / email or Facebook to reserve your space(s) or for specific menu: COOKING CLASSES With Chef, Chris Maher...
Published: 20 January 2012, 1:02 pm
More stories: Read more stories
Custom tabs: View example tabs
...
See More

Like · Comment · Share · January 20 at 2:36pm via Social RSS

Gallery Realty of Taos - A Buyer Brokerage

Changing New Mexico's Image
Taos Real Estate

The image above is from a real estate Facebook page, and the posts you see were not written in Facebook. They were written in the blog for this real estate business. The RSS feed from the blog was placed into one of several Facebook Apps you can get for free, install into your Facebook Page, and then place the RSS URL into the app to get the posts to display.

OK, hopefully you're enough into RSS to understand the basics and that RSS frees us up to write our content at one site, and then have it display on others.

Twitter

While Twitter no longer provides you with an RSS feed URL for your Twitter account posts, there are third party applications that will create one for you. However, Twitter feeds are unreliable, and they keep changing the rules, so you'll just have to do a search on "create Twitter RSS feed" to find out what's working when you're ready.

However, I'm recommending that you not try to feed OUT of Twitter, instead feed INTO Twitter. With the short nature of Twitter posts, they really don't do a lot for you in the social media and on your blogs. However, it's easy using RSS to get your posts out of your blogs, Facebook, and/or Google+ and into a Twitter account.

What you'll want to be careful to do if you're feeding to Twitter is to realize that only the first 140 or so characters of the post, usually including the title, will feed to Twitter. So you want to make sure your title and first sentence make a good headline.

Facebook

Using Facebook apps, you can go in either direction, feeding in or out of Facebook. This means you can decide where you want to do the most writing and then feed to the other locations from there. If you're blogging, you'll probably want to use the blog RSS feed to place your posts into Facebook. However, you can write in Facebook and feed it to your blog, as well.

A caution here that's not just a Facebook thing. Whenever you can go either way, don't get caught in a loop. You want to go one direction only. If you set up your blog to get your Facebook posts, and Facebook to get your blog posts, you might think that you can then write in either location and accomplish your mission. However, you'll now have duplicates at both ends! That's because the feed at each end will output the post when it shows up, so it will go right back to where you wrote it.

Google+

At the time I'm writing this, and probably for a while, you can't feed INTO Google+. What is there will be there either because someone shared it with you, you shared it, or you wrote it. So you won't be duplicating your blog content in Google+ automatically. Of course, you can just take the link to your newest blog post and write a quick Google+ post and place the link in it, and you may want to take that extra step and time.

You can get your content out of Google+ and into your blog or other social media, however. There is a Google+ application, or extension, that will automatically output your content to Facebook and Twitter, but not to a blog.

You might want to install the Google Chrome browser and give it a try, as it's a great and very fast Web browser. I say this because there is an extension for Chrome (probably soon for Firefox as well) that allows you to share your Google+ post with a lot of different networks, including Facebook, Twitter, and LinkedIn.

Gallery Realty of Taos - A Buyer Brokerage

The average depth to water and average well depths in the Taos real estate MLS 40+...
Taos Real Estate

The average depth to water and average well depths in the Taos real estate MLS 40+ areas is of great interest to buyers. This is a high desert area, and there is a concern on the part of buyers to understand the availability of water. Get the New Mexico State Engineer's Offi...
Published: 29 January 2012, 10:21 pm
More stories: Read more stories
Custom tabs: View example tabs
...
See More

Like · Comment · Share · January 30 at 7:48am via Social RSS

Gallery Realty of Taos - A Buyer Brokerage

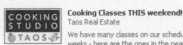
Cooking Classes THIS weekend!
Taos Real Estate

We have many classes on our schedule over the next several weeks - here are the ones in the near future including THIS weekend - hope you can join us! Call 575 776 2665 / email or Facebook to reserve your space(s) or for specific menu: COOKING CLASSES With Chef, Chris Maher...
Published: 20 January 2012, 1:02 pm
More stories: Read more stories
Custom tabs: View example tabs
...
See More

Like · Comment · Share · January 20 at 2:36pm via Social RSS

Gallery Realty of Taos - A Buyer Brokerage

" **Changing New Mexico's Image**
Taos Real Estate

 The image is a screen shot of the download page for the Chrome Extension, called "Extended Share for Google+." Once installed, you can write your post in Google+ and share it with multiple networks, but still not with your blog. I'm getting to that.

In my opinion , Twitter is better suited for incoming feeds, and Google+ is better suited for outgoing feeds. Using RSS, you can syndicate your Google+ posts to your blog. However, if you go to Google+ looking for your RSS feed, you won't find it. Google+ does not support an outgoing feed. However, I'm going to show you how to create one to use. Once you have it, you can use that feed to get your Google+ content into your blog or Facebook, or anywhere else you can display an RSS feed.

Google+ To RSS As A Service

googlePlusUserId : [   ] [Go!]

The image above is all that's on the page at http://gplus-to-rss.
appspot.com/. It's a third party site that will allow you to create
a feed from your Google+ profile. The UserId is there at your
profile or Page profile and is just the last numeric part:
https://plus.google.com/u/0/b/**107441114656642371092/**

I put the number in bold and italics. Just copy out that number
and place it into the box as in the image and click on Go!

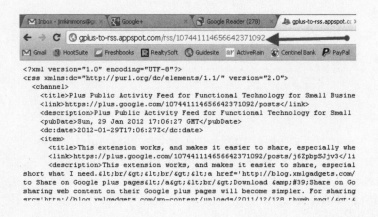

You'll go to that page of XML code, but you don't need that.
All you need is the URL at the top (see the arrow). That's your
newly created RSS feed for that Google+ Business page. When
you enter that into readers, send it into Facebook, or set it up
to show in your blog, your Google+ page posts on that page
will show up.

Recap –Then It Will Be Clearer

I know it seems complicated, but I'll make it easier in a minute with a free online service ($5.99/month for full functions). Right now let's recap the ways you can use RSS or Extensions and plugins to cross-post:

- You can go either way with Facebook: bring in posts or send them out. Facebook provides the RSS URL for outgoing feeds from a Fan Page. You provide an RSS URL to bring posts in.
- Twitter is best for incoming only due to the short nature of Tweets. If you're blogging with WordPress, there are plugins that will automatically post to Twitter. If you're using Google+ or Facebook, there are apps/extensions to send posts to Twitter.
- Google+ doesn't reliably accept incoming posts of any kind at this time, though it's probably coming soon. It's best to do your original posts on Google+ and take them out with the sharing extension I mentioned or with a created RSS feed.
- When an application, extension, or plugin isn't the answer or isn't available, using RSS gets the job done in most cases.

OK, with all of the media, directions and methods I've given you, you're probably wondering how to get it all done. There is an online app called Hootsuite at http://hootsuite.com. It is a dashboard for social media that can help you bring all of this together into one location to display with tabs on your screen.

With Hootsuite, you set up your individual social media accounts and even your blogs all in one place. You can then monitor all of your Twitter feeds, Facebook Pages, Google+ pages, and LinkedIn as well. It's almost a necessity if you're going to be using all of these media and want to do it efficiently without pulling your hair out. The basic account is free, but it only supports a couple of media, so you'll have to go to PRO for $5.99/month. I think you'll find it worth it.

I shrunk the screen down for the shot above, but you can see that there are a number of tabs across the top for social media and a dropdown for the ones that wouldn't show in the smaller window. Also, going to full size with my large monitor, I have five columns displayed, so this dashboard really brings all of your social media to one place where you can monitor it properly.

You can also write a post one time and post to multiple media at once from your dashboard. This isn't something I use often, since I want to do different things in different media, but now and then a quick post with a super sale deal affiliate link can go out right from Hootsuite. Also, there is a link shortener bar under the post so that you can make long links very short in character count.

The real value of Hootsuite is in allowing you to set up your multiple social media accounts and use RSS to cross-post automatically between them from this one application.

The image above shows that once you've entered your different media accounts, you can take RSS feeds from anywhere and feed them to those accounts. The top one in the image is a feed from a blog going to a Facebook account. The other two are Google+ feeds created, as previously mentioned, that are feeding Twitter accounts.

Once you've set these up, they just happen, and you don't have to do anything to have your posts syndicate from and to your various sites, blogs, and social media accounts.

Now envision having a half dozen blogs, Google+, or Facebook pages where you write original content with affiliate links for income. You want to write it once to one of those locations, but then have it automatically appear in all of the other locations, including LinkedIn and Twitter. You can make it all happen with what you've learned in this chapter!

Now if one affiliate link in one place on one site can make you just $5.00 each month, what might you make if that link were now showing up at several other sites? But it's not just about getting an income link displayed as many times as possible. It's about getting your content in front of as many prospect eyes as possible in their favorite social media.

CHAPTER 12

SEO & SEM for Exposure & Income

This chapter is about two different search engine strategies:

- **SEO, Search Engine Optimization** – The design, organization, HTML, and content of a website is optimized to get
better exposure in the free search results pages presented by
the different search engines.

- **SEM, Search Engine Marketing** – Paying for position in the
searches. The paid results are normally displayed at the top
and maybe to the side of the free results.

My purpose here is not to make you a search engine guru, since
I'm not one myself. Actually, many people who advertise that

they are experts and charge for their services are really not able to produce the results they promise. The search engines, and particularly Google, are constantly changing their search algorithms, so those studying what's going on are always behind the most recent developments.

Because there is so much competition for those few, free, first page results positions, many advertisers and some affiliate marketers pay for better position for the keyword searches that bring visitors to their websites and blogs.

In this chapter I'll give you some tips and strategies that are not secrets but are common sense approaches to both SEO and SEM. Let's start with free positions through Search Engine Optimization.

SEO, Search Engine Optimization

Our goal with SEO is to create sites and blogs and to publish content that generates visitors through high positions in the search engines for certain keywords and key phrases. For example, to illustrate the SEO concepts, let's use a camping gear website or blog example. We want to bring visitors to the site with SEO in this section of the chapter.

We know about camping and camping equipment, which is why we chose to build out a site or blog and social media pages to promote our affiliate links with articles and information we write. Because we know our niche, we also know many keywords and phrases that people use to find information and camping products, or just fun camping sites. However, we really need to have a better idea of which words and phrases they use the most as well as variations of those keywords and phrases. This way we can place them properly in our content and site design. The best place to find out is with Google's Keyword

Tool, which you find at https://adwords.google.com/select/KeywordToolExternal

There are so many items and categories of camping gear, so let's just focus in one category for our example. We're going to narrow it down to camping and cooking. Here are some things we might think about for keywords and phrases:

- camp cooking
- camp stoves
- camp dishware
- camping stoves
- camp meals

There are more, but let's start with "camp cooking" to show how to use Google's Keyword Tool.

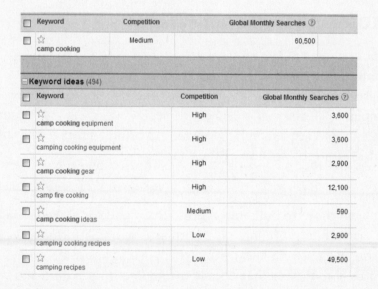

Keyword	Competition	Global Monthly Searches ⑦
☆ camp cooking	Medium	60,500

Keyword ideas (494)

Keyword	Competition	Global Monthly Searches ⑦
☆ camp cooking equipment	High	3,600
☆ camping cooking equipment	High	3,600
☆ camp cooking gear	High	2,900
☆ camp fire cooking	High	12,100
☆ camp cooking ideas	Medium	590
☆ camping cooking recipes	Low	2,900
☆ camping recipes	Low	49,500

The image shows a search I did with the Google Keyword Tool on "camp cooking." It's a partial screen, and only a few results of a much longer list of are shown. However, let's see what information we can get from this search.

We see that the phrase "camp cooking" gets around 60,500 searches per month on Google. The statement that it has "Medium" Competition refers to those who pay for position (SEM) and the competitive nature of the bidding for the key phrase. It does tell us something about the difficulty we may have in getting high free positioning, as well.

However, look at some of the other results to see other phrases we can use in our content to draw people to our site or blog. Look particularly at "camping recipes." It gets a lot of searches, 49,500, and has low competition.

So let's say we have a post on our blog or one or more articles on our site, each with a camping cooking recipe or text about camp cooking and recipes. We will probably have affiliate links to recipe books, but we can also display some text links and image ads to cookware and camp food items alongside our article references,. By focusing on the "camping recipes" key phrase, we can optimize that post or article page for that phrase and increase our chance of better search position.

Make liberal use of the Google Keyword Tool to learn the words and phrases people are using in relation to your affiliate marketing niche. Print out these reports and use the key phrases as ideas for blog posts or articles focused on each of them. You can optimize for more than one keyword or phrase in an article or post, so feel free to do so.

Optimizing for Keywords and Phrases

Now we are writing some content around the "camping recipes" phrase, so what do we do to incorporate it for the best results? These are not "guru" tips, but everyday things that will help your content in the search engines if you get into the habit of using them. For the content itself, use your key phrase:

- in the article or post title
- in the first sentence of the post or article
- throughout the article when appropriate
- with bold, italic and larger fonts or bullets if possible
- in the last sentence

That's it for the content itself. It's not rocket science and not a guarantee, but over time these tips have worked for many.

META

If you're into the HTML behind the scenes, or more often your website or blog platform offers you the ability to enter your META information, here's what that looks like.

```
<head>
<title>Stats about all US cities - real estate, relocation info, house prices, home value
photos, education, maps, weather, houses, schools, neighborhoods, and more</title>
<meta name="Description" content="Stats about all US cities - real estate, relocation info
race, income, photos, education, crime, weather, houses, etc.">
<meta http-equiv="Content-Language" content="en">
<meta name="robots" content="index, follow">
<link rel="stylesheet" type="text/css" href="http://pics3.city-data.com/css/style.css">
<style type="text/css"> html .fb_share_link ( padding:2px 0 0 20px; height:16px;
background:url(http://static.ak.facebook.com/images/share/facebook_share_icon.gif?6:26981;
<script language="javascript" type="text/javascript" src="http://pics3.city-data.com/js/s
</head>
```

In the head section of the web page, we see the <title> meta tag first, then the Description section. These are areas where many site back-end software packages simply take what you wrote and places it there automatically. However, WordPress and many website services allow you to enter different meta information into a box when you're writing the content. I wanted to show you this because, if you are given a chance to view and change it, you may want to adjust it a bit to have your key phrase in the meta areas. Some will also have a <keywords> meta section.

Backlinks

The other piece of SEO is working to get as many quality links back to your site from other sites around the Web. Blogging sometimes makes this easier, as bloggers tend to link to other similar blogs a lot, with a special section on many blogs just for links.

Don't try to take a shortcut with some "link-building" scheme or paid service, since Google has those figured out. You may actually do more harm than good. You want to link to other sites when appropriate, which will slowly get their site owners to notice your good will and reciprocate voluntarily.

Another thing I'll mention in some chapters to come is how you can go out and write comments on other sites or blogs, or how you can write articles or guest posts on other sites that allow you to link back to your site.

SEO is complex, but the way to think about it in your daily activities is that you want great content written around your relevant keywords and phrases, and you want other sites linking to that content to give it a vote of confidence. Over time there will be a cumulative effect if you stick to these simple and easy-to-implement strategies.

SEM, Search Engine Marketing

SEO is free, unless you pay for the services of a guru. SEM, Search Engine Marketing, is getting your position in the search results by paying for it. This isn't something a beginner affili-ate marketer should attempt. Once you have your blogs, sites and social media marketing working, you may want to allot a certain portion of your income to SEM.

The major thrust of SEM marketing my most users is PPC, Pay-Per-Click marketing. This means that you as an advertiser/pub-lisher pay the search engine only when a searcher sees your ad in the display results, clicks on it, and comes to your site landing page.

You only pay for results, but results may not pay you. That click and visit to your blog or website full of affiliate links will not result in income unless the visitor actually clicks on one of those affiliate links. So there are several things that need to be in place before you risk spending money on clicks to your site.

The Content of the Page They Land On
This is critical. Let's say you're running a paid ad in search that is promoting your fitness or health site or blog. I'll get into ad text when I show you examples in Google Adwords, but for now let's say that our ad is trying to promote a specific page with a single product featured, perhaps a dietary supplement.

You don't want to take the paid click visitor to your home page at the site or blog. If you're promoting a specific supplement in the ad, then the page where they land should feature that product prominently, at the very least, even if other similar products are there as well. The visitor is expecting to find what the ad promised.

An Effective Call to Action
Don't assume that the visitor came there specifically to buy the product. They may want information, and you should have that information on the page. However, a call to action should also be very prominently displayed. You must tell them to click here for a free trial, click here to purchase at the sale price, or something that tells them what you want them to do.

Money Wasted
Many times I hear people talking about how they tried SEM and it didn't work. They spent a lot of money and didn't sell much, wasting their advertising dollars. It's common, first because they ignored the two things I just told you. Also, they didn't do enough research or have a realistic expectation for their ability

to convert visitors to income.

If you're getting $15.00 for a click for a free trial of a high ticket exercise video product, you can't just say that you can pay $1.00/click for search engine clicks. You would only break even if you get one trial for every 15 clicks. And you can probably expect your conversions to be more like one in 50 or less. That's how you lose money, getting $15 for every $50 you spend.

Be Realistic and Test With a Small Budget

When I show you how Google Adwords works, this will be more clear. However, you're going to be paying a certain price for each click. You will not have any idea of how well your site will convert from click visitors to affiliate income, so you must move cautiously. Set a small test budget and be ready to cut it off immediately or adjust as necessary to assure that you're making a profit through conversions.

Google AdWords

I'm only going to use Google AdWords as an example, as Yahoo Search marketing and others are very similar. Google is the big player anyway, with far more clicks and revenue than all of the others.

New Ad Campaign Setup

Once you have your account set up with Google AdWords, you can set up your first ad campaign.

Select campaign settings

Load settings ⑦   Campaign type ▾   or   Existing campaign ▾

General

Campaign name   Fitness Videos

Locations and Languages

Locations ⑦   In what geographical locations do you want your ads to appear?
○ All countries and territories
◉ United States and Canada
○ United States
○ Let me choose...
Enter a location such as a city, region, or country   Show map

Select campaign settings

Load settings ⑦   [Campaign type ▼]   or   [Existing campaign ▼]

General

Campaign name   [Fitness Videos]

Locations and Languages

Locations ⑦   In what geographical locations do you want your ads to appear?
○ All countries and territories
◉ United States and Canada
○ United States
○ Let me choose...
[Enter a location such as a city, region, or country]   Show map

We'll name this campaign "Fitness Videos," and leave the default for the U.S. and Canada for the ads to be displayed. You may want to further restrict visibility to just the U.S., or if later you're marketing area-specific products and services, you can choose geographic exposure areas.

Networks and devices

Networks ⑦   ○ All available sites (Recommended for new advertisers)
◉ Let me choose...
Search   ☑ Google search
☑ Search partners (requires Google search)
Display   ☑ Display Network ⑦
◉ Broad reach: Show ads on pages that match my primary targeting method ⑦
Example: Show ads if keywords match
○ Specific reach: Show ads only on pages that match all my targeting methods ⑦
Example: Show ads only if both keywords and placements match

Devices ⑦   ◉ All available devices (Recommended for new advertisers)
○ Let me choose...

In this next section, you can get fooled by Google. The "All available sites" is checked and it says that it's recommended for new advertisers. Change to "Let me choose," and you'll see some stuff appear underneath.

This is where you find that there are two networks, the Search network and the "Display" network. Once you know more about the Display Network and have some experience with this system, you may want to do both, but for now it's much easier for you to learn and safer for your budgeting if you stick to just displaying your ads when people are on search pages.

Next we set up our money stuff. Leave the manually set bids box checked, as you'll want to set your precise bid for clicks yourself. However, the Default bid box will set this amount if you forget or don't set a specific bid amount for each keyword combination. Keep this low, maybe $0.25, since you don't want any surprises, and you plan on setting your own bids, anyway. The Budget per day is the most you want to spend each calendar day, and this is how you control your spending precisely.

Now this doesn't mean that if you put $3.00 in there you'll never spend more than $3.00 per day. The last click of the day can carry you over just a bit, maybe to $3.15 or so just because you were under on the previous click and went over with the last click.

Now you're seeing one of the values of this type of marketing. You set a budget that is automatically maintained for you, and you only spend money when you get that visitor to your site.

In the image above, we're building our first ad to run in this campaign. We can build groups of ads, so we'll name this group Fitness Ads Group 1.

Then we set our ad title and text.
- **Title** – Fitness Videos that Work
- **Text** – Users swear by these fitness videos Guaranteed better health & bodies.
- **Display URL** – Particularly if you have a URL that's not pretty or doesn't get across what's at the landing page, you can have a different URL in the ad display than where you're actually taking the searcher.
- **Destination URL** – This is your landing page URL where the searcher will land when they click on the ad.

Google strongly advises, and I agree, that you try to work the keywords you're bidding on into your ad title and text. This is because they will automatically be **bolded.** This makes your ad stand out with the very words they typed in their search, and that usually means more clicks, and a better CTR, Click-Through-Ratio.

You can see the ad previews below to see how they'll display based on where they're going to show up, and I'll get into that positioning in this chapter, as well. Top ads are the ones that Google deems to be the best and gives them priority, while the side ads are lower in their priority and ranked from top to bottom by Google for display.

Obviously, you want your ad to be as close to the very top #1 slot as *affordably* possible. I'll get into that in a moment, since I do quite well with ads not in the top three on the left but at the top on the side to the right, and I pay a lot less.

Keywords
_____

⊟ Select keywords
Your ad can show on Google when people search for the keywords you choose here. These keywords will also
automatically find relevant sites on the Display Network to show your ads.

When creating your keyword list, think like your customers: how would they describe your products or services?
Specific keywords (often containing 2-3 words) will help you show your ads to the most interested users. Try
starting with 10-20 keywords. You can always expand or refine later.Help me choose effective keywords.

Enter one keyword per line. Add keywords by spreadsheet

Help me choose effective keywords.

No sample keywords available.

[Re-estimate search traffic]

Estimated traffic summary ⑦
The following are approximations for the keywords above.
Based on max CPC: and budget: **$3.00/day**.

Avg. CPC: $1.35 - $1.65

Clicks/day: 2 - 2

Cost/day: ⑦ $2.70 - $3.30

Once you've set up the ad, we tell Google the keywords we're
going to bid on. We may do more than just one phrase and
probably will. However, for this example, we'll just put in "fitness videos." You can go back to our discussion of the Keyword
Tool to find others to bid on, as well.

Notice that Google is telling us that the average CPC, Cost
Per Click, being paid for this keyword phrase is $1.35 to
$1.65, and that our daily budget will only get us two clicks
per day. We can change our budget if we want more clicks.
Now you know the basics of setting up a campaign and
an ad. There's much more involved in managing a Google
AdWords account and multiple campaigns, but you have the
basics necessary to get started when and if you decide to do
PPC advertising.

I did a search on "fitness videos," and here are the search results. The top three results to the left are paid ads, while all of the ads on the right side are paid ads, too. Ads under the first three on the left are the free results, achieved with good SEO. Notice that several ads have **Fitness Videos** in bold, and they tend to stand out from the others. The BeachBody® ad on the left is a paid ad without the bold keywords and is probably less effective with a lower CTR.

CTR, Click-Through-Ratio – the percentage of clicks based on impressions, the number of times your ad is displayed.

100 displays with 5 clicks means 5/100 = .05 or 5% CTR

What I'm about to tell you now is probably the most important thing you need to know before starting any SEM type advertising, especially on Google.

Your <u>Ad Score</u> is the Major Factor in Your Budget!

Google uses a scoring system to determine where your ad will show up. Wait, you say! Won't I be on top if I make the highest bid? Won't my bid for each click determine where my ad appears at the top or on the right side? NOPE, not forever anyway. This is where your ad's quality score comes in.

When you first set up an ad and a bid-per-click, that's all Google has to go on for performance. So yes, your ad will be placed mostly based on those factors. However, here's what happens after that:

- As your ad is shown (impressions), people begin to click on it.
- A CTR, Click-Through-Ratio begins right away to be computed by Google, and the more times the ad shows and the more times it's clicked on, the higher the CTR can be if people respond to the ad.
- Google checks out your landing page and scores it like it would for SEO based on how relevant the content of the landing page is to the wording of the ad.
- A whole bunch of other secret ingredients are blended and your Ad Score is computed.

Your ad score is continuously changing based on these factors, but it begins to be somewhat consistent and can then be compared to the ad scores of your competitor bidders, those ads that are above and below yours.

Google wants people who click on these ads to find what they want so they'll keep using Google Search. And Google would rather get 100 clicks paying them $0.10/click than 10 clicks paying $1.00 each. It's the same $10.00, but with 90 more satisfied searchers.

So the ad score becomes the major ranking factor. And *higher ad scores will move your ad up in the rankings above competi-*

tors who pay more per click but have lower CTRs and lower ad scores!

Read that again, because it's true and can save you a LOT of money over time, not to mention get more traffic that will make you more money, as well. I've started campaigns that indicated I'd have to bid more than $2.00 per click to get decent rankings.

However, within a very short time, sometimes days to a week, my CTRs and ad scores were higher than competitors' because I did everything right. Suddenly I was only paying $1.50/click, then $0.90/click, then $0.55/click! But at the same time my ad was moving up in the results.

Now you have the basics of SEO and SEM, so you can begin to put together your marketing plan and build your affiliate marketing income flow.

CHAPTER 13

Article Marketing, Forums, & Commenting

This isn't a long chapter, but it's an important one. We've covered SEO, and one of the things discussed was links back to your sites and blogs to give them better search engine positioning on your best keywords and phrases for your niche or products. Also, what you'll read here is just as valuable for knowing where you can place actual direct affiliate links rather than just trying to link to your sites.

Forums & Blog Commenting

I'm grouping forums and blog commenting together because they're both about online discussions and your ability to join in. Whether you're commenting on another blog or joining the discussion on a forum related to your product or service niche, you'll be adding your voice to the discussion with multiple goals:

- Linking back from your forum post or blog comment to your own site or blog.
- Entering a direct affiliate link for income.
- Building a presence in a forum group or in the blogging community to help with your credibility and position yourself as a good information resource.

You Need to Be There Anyway

If you're going to be marketing to a niche, you'll need to be keeping up with what's going on in that niche. You'll want to know about new things happening and new products or vendor/advertisers you may want to work with. So you'll be reading related blogs and monitoring discussions in niche-related forums.

If you're going to be there anyway, join in the discussions and use them to accomplish the marketing tasks I bulleted above. Some will have rules about affiliate links, many will not, but abide by all rules and be a good site citizen. At the same time, take advantage of what you are allowed to do in the way of linking.

Always try to place your links in text that's informative and not a direct sales pitch. If you're answering a question about your niche, one approach is to do that in brief and then link to your site with "I've written more about this here." Your answer will be appreciated, and you should have the link actually take them to more detailed information at your site or blog even if there are affiliate links on the page.

Forums are everywhere, and people love to talk about their hobbies and interests. Back to our camping example:

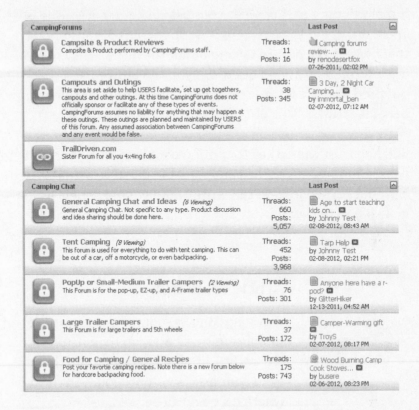

Take a look at the bottom one in the image. It's about Food
for Camping / General Recipes. You can't find a better place to
promote our camping food and recipe products and books.
Here's an example of just a few of many forums about fitness
and exercise:

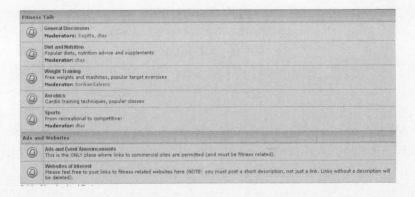

It really doesn't matter what your product or service niche is. There are going to be dozens if not hundreds of forums out there where people are talking about the niche. They're sharing information, asking questions you can answer, and checking out products and services recommended by other forum members they trust.

Building trust will be key to getting people to click your affiliate links in forums. It's particularly valuable if you've actually used a product or service and can write about your experience with it, a kind of review.

EzineArticles.com

GoArticles.com

ArticleDashboard.com

SearchWarp.com

ArticlesBase.com

iSnare.com *

SelfGrowth.com

Buzzle.com

ArticleCity.com

IdeaMarketers.com

ArticleAlley.com

Web-Source.net

SelfSEO.com

Amazines.com

Article Marketing

The image shows some of the top article submission sites based on their actual visitor traffic. After all, if you want to benefit from your article writing, you want it to be where it's going to be seen.

An added benefit is SEO, as you can link to your sites and blogs from these articles, creating a back-link for search engine credit. If you do a Google search on "article submission sites," you'll find that there are hundreds. Sometimes overall traffic isn't as important as targeted traffic. If you find an article submission site focused on your product marketing niche, it could be a better placement for some articles.

Maybe you're selling information products, and some are about SEO, so you could place an article at SelfSEO.com with some tips and a link to your site or blog with affiliate links.

How Article Sites Work

I'll use one of the largest, EzineArticles.com, to give you an idea of how these sites work.

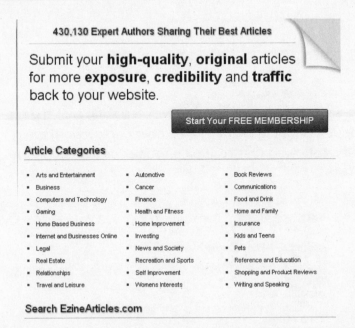

The image is from the home page at the site, and you can see the major categories for articles published there. For our example, let's go back to Camping. I went to the Travel & Leisure category link to get this dropdown:

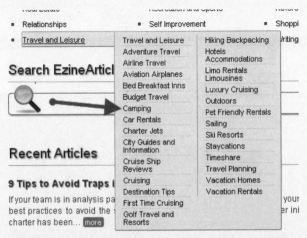

There I found a Camping category, so let's see what we find.

Camping and My Favorite Campfire Recipe
by Roger Dale Lee
Camping in a travel trailer and cooking over a camp fire can not be beat. I love making this recipe when I am camping.

What to Bring When Family Camping - A Few Things To Never Forget
by Richard Ethridge
Everybody likes to go on a family camping trip once in a while. Not only does it get you away from your job and the daily grind of your life, but it also takes you away from the city, and all of the artificial and completely unnatural things in the world. But what do you need to do when you go camping? Well, here are a few things you'll want to make sure you never forget.

We will never sell or rent your email address [Subscribe]

📶 Camping RSS Feed

🔒 Top Authors in Camping

More Travel and Leisure categories:

Travel and Leisure (26,246)
Adventure Travel (6,572)

There are a great many articles, but it's interesting that the top one is about a camping recipe. Remember our keyword research earlier showed that "camping recipes" is a great phrase to work with.

Author Spotlight

Elliot Zovighian
💎 Diamond Author
131 Articles

Elliot Zovighian is a Certified Development Strategist, writer, and speaker from Toronto, Canada. His purpose is to educate and teach people how to... more

Linda K Murdock
💎 Diamond Author
35 Articles

Linda Murdock is the author of four books including the best-seller A Busy Cook's Guide to Spices and her newest, A Busy Cook's Guide to... more

Matthew A. Boreau
💎 Diamond Author
23 Articles

Matthew Alexander Boreau is the original Dwarf Hamster Whisperer. He has been fascinated with dwarf hamsters for as long as he can remember. To... more

Alan Stratton
💎 Diamond Author
36 Articles

With today's internet tools and communication possibilities, Alan Stratton CPA CMA brings the benefit of his cost management and computer systems... more

The article at the link is written by the owner of an RV dealer-ship, so the links he placed were to his dealership site. This could just as easily be an article you write about a favorite recipe with links to others that are direct affiliate links to camping recipe books or links to camping gear for cooking.

Lest you wonder about how narrow of a niche you can write about and find value here, check out the third writer down in this Author Spotlight box on the site's home page.

He writes about dwarf hamsters. Now that's a niche. He may not be an affiliate marketer, but he's deriving some value from writing for this site, probably links to his own site or blog.

The idea is to write articles that position you as an expert that is very knowledgeable in your marketing niche.

The image above shows the EzineArticles.com pitch as to why you should want to write articles for the site. You position yourself as an expert and get links back to your site or blog. This site doesn't allow direct affiliate linking. In fact, you can only link back to the home page of a site that you own. You can't link internally to product or landing pages. However, writ-ing an article or two for this site with a link will not take too long and can bring you traffic for years to come.

At the time of this writing, one major article site that appears to allow direct affiliate linking is GoArticles.com. You should read the rules, though. One statement explains that links in the article should "support the content of the article." I would suppose that a link with anchor text of "go here to buy the best fitness video ever" may not be approved. While the same link may be approved if linking to exactly the same affiliate link but saying "fitness videos should provide exercises for the intended age & body condition group."

However, GoArticles.com states clearly that promotional product links can be placed in the Author Bio, so you can definitely place some of your best niche affiliate links there. If you write a great informative article, many will check out your author bio for credibility.

This chapter outlines ways in which you can promote yourself, your sites, and your blogs, and place direct affiliate links in many cases. The Web is a great marketplace for the small business person because of these linking strategies.

CHAPTER 14

Repeat Business With Email Marketing

This entire book is about placing affiliate links around the Web and enjoying an amazing income when people click on them and take the appropriate action. Well, those same links can be placed in an email, too, and sometimes the CTR from email is higher.

When might you want to market with email? If your market niche(s) are such that you can provide ongoing information of value to a list of email subscribers, you could find email marketing to be a really profitable business. Let's use our tried-and-true camping niche example. If you're maintaining a blog or website about camping, you can offer some premium information via a report or eBook that will be delivered by email.

When the prospect fills out the online form to get the information, you get their email address for future marketing.

If your niche is camping and you know a lot about it, you could write up a special report or mini-eBook about the top 25 camping spots in the country or some other topic that's easily researched on the Web. If you can't spell or don't want to write the report, you can go to sites like Elance.com or Guru.com and hire writers very inexpensively to write one for you. I've seen bids on those sites to create eBooks for as little as $50 to $100. Once your eBook or report is created, make sure you get it into the PDF format. Don't send out MS Word or other formats because too many people will have trouble opening them. 95+% of all computers come with the Adobe PDF reader free software which will be able to open your files.

So let's say that we've created our little eBook about the top campsites and have it ready to deliver in exchange for their name and email address. You'll need a form on your website or blog to collect their information, and you'll need a mechanism to automatically deliver the report immediately, 24/7/365, no matter what you're doing.

After that free delivery, you'll then want to set up your marketing to follow-up with emails in the future, each with a camping topic of interest and affiliate links to products that fit into the email topic. Let's see how those might look.

Email Auto-responder & Ongoing Marketing

The first email to go out is the one that delivers the free report or eBook they requested. You'll want to keep this email short and simple, mostly thanking them and giving them the link to the report if you have it stored on your site or have it attached to the email.

It's better to use a link and have the report somewhere on your site or blog server, since there won't be problems with email systems not accepting the attachment for spam reasons or because of a large file. You can learn from your site host or blog host how to upload the file and link to it.

That first email, due to the automatic nature of delivery, is called an "auto-responder." I'll give you some resources later in this chapter to take care of this task, as well as deliver future emails on a timed basis. This is called "drip email." While you could just write your emails when necessary and manually deliver them to each new signup, it's going to be too much work and take too much of your time. You'll want to do drip email, and I'll give you the resources here, as well. Right now, how might our email series look?

1. Maybe a few days or a week after the report/eBook delivery, this email goes out with the title *Gourmet Camp Cooking Made Easy.* You have a great book product that you promote, and you take some of the information from the introduction that sells it and put that in the email, then the affiliate link.

2. Maybe a week or so after that email, another one goes out with a title like *Safety at the Campsite.* You have affiliate links to food storage containers that keep the food odors contained so they don't attract wildlife. You take some of their promotional text and put it into the email and, of course, the affiliate links.

3. Do as many of these follow-up emails as you can build, and you'll find that you're selling to the same customers over and over. You might even pick up some new business when they forward the emails to their friends.

But wait! How do we make this process automatic and pain-less? We sign up for an email marketing service that handles all of this for you, including maintaining your email list and follow-ing all of the legal stuff about unsubscribes.

MailChimp.com

There are a number of drip email marketing online services, and you should do your own research about them to find which one you prefer. However, I'll take you through MailChimp's service, as you may even be able to get by at the free level, and it will do everything we've discussed so far.

You're going to use a service like this to create your online form to put on your site. Then you'll create the single auto-respond-er email to deliver your report or eBook. Finally, you're going to write your series of emails, tell MailChimp when each should go out, then let the service do the work. This is called a "cam-paign."

When someone comes to your site or blog and sends in the form, their name and email address will be placed into the ap-propriate list. You can have several email campaigns for dif-ferent purposes and niche markets, and you'll have a list and series of emails for each. When a new prospect hits the list, the auto-responder delivers their document, and the service sends all future emails out on the schedule you set up.

Get Started With MailChimp in 3 Simple Steps

Create A Subscriber List   Design Signup Forms   Create & Send A Campaign

The image shows that you'll be creating a subscriber list for your camping campaign, then designing a form to collect subscribers for your list from your website or blog. Finally, you design and write your emails. It's a simple process and one you only do once. Once those emails are built and the form is in place, you just sit back and let the income roll in.

Your first step is to set up your list to which subscribers will be added with the form you'll design next.

There are fields to name your list, as well as a FROM name & address to have an automated response go out to let them know they've successfully signed up.

You also create your signature for the bottom of each email, with your name, company, email, website, phone or other information.

Now we're designing our form to place on the website or blog. Once we get it designed, we'll be presented with the HTML code to paste into our site where we want the form to display. You can create a number of form fields to gather information, but in most cases you want to keep it limited to name and email. Asking for much more information turns people off, and you get nothing.

So the first three fields in this form are what I'd recommend you use in most cases.

The last step, and the one that takes the longest and has the greatest number of steps, is the creation of your email series. You create one autoresponder as discussed to deliver the report/ eBook. Then you write each email and place your affiliate links into it.

You get to choose from a number of email style and color templates to give your emails the right look. All you have to do is to write them and set up the schedule for automated delivery. This is done by telling MailChimp how many days should pass between each delivery.

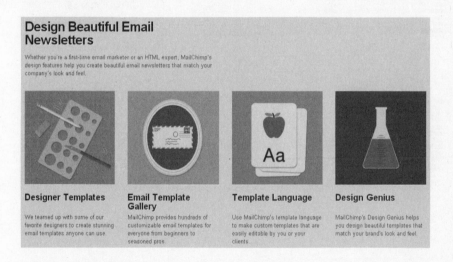

The image shows the information about their email templates and design features.

There are plenty of other services you can check out. A search on "drip email campaign software" turned up hundreds of results, the first few of which are shown here

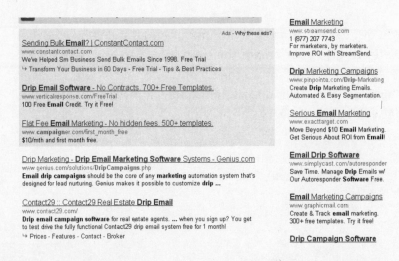

Email marketing can expand your business and increase your income dramatically. If you market related niche products, you can even cross over and add people to other lists.

CHAPTER 15

Affiliate Marketing on Facebook

Where do 800+ million people spend a huge amount of their time online? On Facebook, of course. And it's the biggest on-going conversation place in the world. Where people talk and gather, there's money to be made. And when they do it online, there's affiliate profits to be made, as well.

Placing Your Links in Discussions

The simplest and quickest way to get started is to just place your affiliate links into discussions you find on Facebook. How do you find those discussions? It's really easy. You just use the Search box at the top of the page. I entered "camping" and got this dropdown:

Notice that the top result is for those people who in their pro-files entered that they are interested in camping.

And there are more than seven million of those people! At the time of this search, more than 170,000 discussions were going on about camping.

We also see choices for fan pages about camping, like the Camping Gear Outlet and Survival Camping World. All of these locations are places to find people with an interest in camping.

Once you find people and discussions, you can join in and place affiliate links where they fit into the discussion and will not be perceived as outright selling.

Going to some of the fan pages for companies, perhaps even companies you are an affiliate rep for, you will find people commenting. They're potential "friend" candidates to begin to build out your contact list for placing your links.

The image shows a fan page for an RV company, and you can see an individual commenting on one of their posts.

Just keep interacting, answering questions, and joining in discussions, placing your links wherever they fit and you'll eventually begin to build a following and get your clicks and income.

Build Your Own Fan Page

That American RV page is a good example. You could build a page for your camping niche, maybe name it "Everything Camping," or whatever good name is available that fits the niche and will get you to show up in Facebook searches.

Having your own page is a whole different situation, since you're clearly selling, and you're going to try to build your own list of friends and those who follow your page as fans. You'll be trying to post things that get "Liked" which gets them into the streams of the friends of those who like your page.

Create a Page
Create a Facebook Page to build a closer relationship with your audience and customers.

Local Business or Place

Company, Organization or Institution

Brand or Product

Artist, Band or Public Figure

Entertainment

Cause or Community

At the bottom of Facebook pages, you will find a link to "Create a Page." Clicking on it takes you to the screen you see above. We're going to create a page about camping to market our camping products, so probably the best choice is the "Brand or Product" button. When we click on it, we fill in our data:

The closest category for our use is Outdoor Gear/Sporting Goods, and I placed our Brand to be Everything Camping.

Then we agree to the terms and click on Get Started to begin building our fan page for promoting our affiliate links and ads.

Once we move on, we'll be doing a bit of setup for our page:

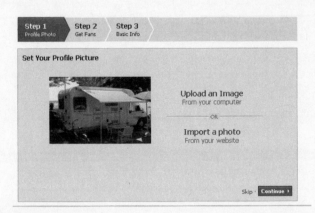

The image shows the step where we upload an image that represents our niche well, as many times the eye of the Facebook user will be drawn to an image before they read any text.

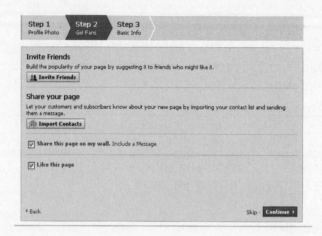

The image shows the next step as it comes up in the display. However, I recommend that you uncheck the Share and Like buttons at the bottom. I don't know why Facebook presents these at this point, since the page needs some content before we share it. And you can do this sharing later at any time. The last step is in the next image:

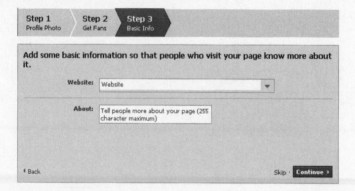

We can enter a website or blog, if we have one for this niche, and describe our niche and page. I'm not going to go through with the final step, but when you click on Continue you will see your page, ready for you to upload some images, enter your first status update, and do a great many other things to get started with your marketing.

Once your page has some content, share it with everyone you know and promote it on your website or blog. Start writing great content updates with good information, add links to great camping sites and information, and, of course, place your affiliate links where appropriate.

A Facebook fan page isn't going to produce results overnight. However, over time those who Like your page will be recommending it to their friends, and this effect will multiply. You'll build an audience for your informative posts in your niche and you'll get clicks and income from your affiliate linking.

Facebook Ads

I'm not going to go into a lot of detail about Facebook Ads, but you may want to consider them in the future, though I don't recommend them for the new affiliate marketer. Get your fan page(s) up, and fill them with good content and affiliate links first.

However, if you decide that there are some really great paying affiliate products that you want to get in front of Facebook users interested in your niche, Facebook ads may be the way to do that.

Be very careful, though. In our discussion of SEM, Search Engine Marketing, we learned that you're going to only have a certain percentage of people whose click you paid for that will go ahead and take the desired action on your landing page. The same applies here.

If you're promoting one of your landing pages that features camping or fitness products with a Facebook Ad, you're going to pay Facebook when you get the click to your site. Many of the visitors will not end up taking the action that gets you paid, so you'll need to factor that into your marketing plan and budget.

I want you to know about Facebook Ads because you can do more to target who sees your ad than in almost any other type of marketing, including SEM. Facebook allows you to focus on the users most likely to have an interest in your products or services in such a way that any clicks you get will definitely be from someone with an expressed interest in your niche.

Let's see how that works by setting up a sample ad for a page where we feature camping cooking gear and recipes.

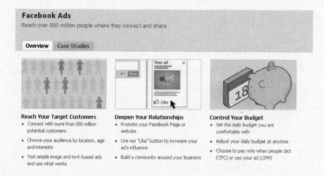

 As the image shows, you can reach a very highly-targeted group of people with Facebook Ads, and you can control your budget just like we did by setting a daily budget amount in our Google AdWords example in the SEO and SEM chapter.

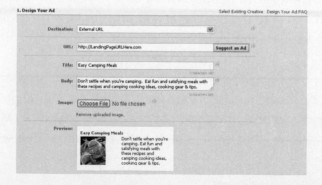

The image above is the first section of the page where we con-
struct our Facebook Ad. We're going to take the person who
clicks to a page with a couple of great recipes for free, but with
affiliate links to camping cookbooks as well as cooking utensils
and gear.

This section is where we place our URL for our landing page, as
well as title, text, and image for our ad.

The image above shows how we can drill down through the
user base and target those with specific interests in our niche.
You can just keep adding keywords or restrict those who see
the ad to fewer people with a more focused interest.

3. Campaigns, Pricing and Scheduling

Campaign & Budget

Campaign Name: My Ads

Budget (USD): $3.00 daily budget

Create a new campaign

Schedule

Campaign Schedule: 05/14/2011 10:28am – Ongoing

Pricing

○ Pay for Impressions (CPM)

◉ Pay for Clicks (CPC)

Max Bid (USD). How much are you willing to pay per click? (min 0.01 USD)

0.99   Suggested Bid: 0.62 - 1.43 USD

Note: Tax is not included in the bids, budgets and other amounts shown.
Use Suggested Bid (Simple Mode)

[Place Order] [Review Ad]

This last image shows how we can set up our daily budget, as well as the amount we're willing to pay for each click.

Again, it's very important that you have a realistic outlook for your conversion rate of click-through actions for those who then click on one of your affiliate links and then click to buy. That's three steps they must take before you get paid.

So you may be paying only $0.25/click to get them to your landing page. However, they then must click one of your affiliate links to go somewhere else. THEN they must take the action your vendor/advertiser wants them to take before you get paid. Sometimes this works better if you're building an email list because you can take them to a page with your recipes and affiliate links but also to a form they can submit for a series of recipes to follow. Your email series becomes those recipes. You can then place affiliate links in every email. They are sometimes more likely to give up their email address for future free stuff than they may be to buy on that first-click visit.

That's a basic Facebook affiliate marketing primer. You have enough information to start placing your marketing on Facebook and tracking results to decide what works best for you.

CHAPTER 16
Google+ for Affiliate Marketing

Google+ is less than a year old as I write this. However, in just months this new social network has signed up more than 100 million members. When it was "by invitation only" at the start, it reached ten million members in just 16 days. It took Twitter and Facebook both more than two years to do that.

Google+ includes some of the best features of Twitter and Facebook but is different in many ways. For our affiliate marketing activities, we're going to create pages much like we did in Facebook. In Google+ your pages must be created from your personal profile, but they're not connected back to it as they are in Facebook. So you can have multiple business entities as pages and they will not all be linked out of one place. You can be your own competitor as it were.

How Google+ Works

Let's take a look at how Google+ works, particularly Circles and Business Pages.

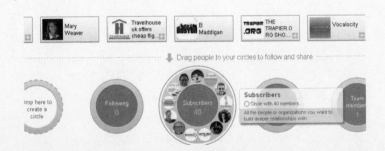

The image shows the main feature of Google+ that's very different from Facebook. You communicate with people on Google+ much the same way you do in real life. Some things you want to tell to some people or groups, and other things you want to tell to a different person or group. And you don't necessarily want those different groups to see what you've communicated to others.

With Google+ Circles, you place people and contacts into specific Circles, kind of like membership in clubs. When you post something in your personal Google+ profile, you can share it publicly for the world to see, or you can pick and choose Circles to see it. So, if you have a Family Circle, Friends Circle, and Job Circle, you can post work-related stuff to the Job Circle, but things you may not want your boss to see to your Family and/or Friends Circles.

You must have a personal profile with Google+ and it needs to be your real name. So I don't recommend using that profile for your affiliate marketing activities and trying to group market niches into Circles. Though you can do that, it can become quite difficult to figure out where a particular person came from to get them into the proper Circle for future marketing.

Google+ Business Pages

About Google+ Pages

Google+ Pages provides businesses, products, brands, and organizations with a public identity and presence on Google+. Pages can currently be created for one of five categories to help guide you when signing up:

1. Product or Brand
2. Company, Institution or Organization
3. Local Business or Place
4. Arts, Entertainment or Sports
5. Other

Google+ pages interact in the Google+ world similar to the way that regular Google+ profile owners do - they can add people to circles, edit their profile, share things in Google+, +1 comments and photos, and create and join Hangouts. But they're not entirely the same. Learn about how pages and profiles are different.

> ✓ If you're unsure whether you're viewing a page or an individual's profile, look for the Google+ Pages icon 🔲 next to the name at the top of the page.

The image shows what Google+ says about pages. You can see that there are similarities with Facebook Fan Pages, especially the categorization of the page business type. You get great help from Google and should have no problem setting up pages. There are differences in what you can do with a page and how a page interacts in Google+ with other users.

Differences between Google+ Pages and Google+ Profiles

Pages are extremely similar to profiles, but they have some key differences:

- Pages can't add people to circles until the page is added first or mentioned. Learn more.
- Pages can be made for a variety of different entities whereas profiles can only be made for people.
- Pages can have multiple administrators.
- The default privacy setting for elements on your page profile is public.
- Pages have the +1 button.
- Pages can't +1 other pages, nor can they +1 stuff on the Web.
- Pages can't play games.
- Pages don't have the option to share to 'Extended circles'.
- Pages can't hangout on a mobile device.
- Local pages have special fields that help people find the business' physical location. Learn more about local pages.

The image shows what Google+ says about these differences. The major one that slows the growth of your interactions is that you can't add people to your Page Circles like you can with a personal profile. You can only add them after they add you. This is a logical deterrent to spamming, but you'll have to be more creative to get followers.

You can't even comment on someone's post on Google+ as your page unless they're already in one of that page's Circles. So, you'll have to take your page and do a lot of great informative writing about your niche, link to your websites or blogs, and you'll begin to show up in people's streams because they're

Stream

Demo post where you would write about your favorite great camping recipe. You may even provide one complete recipe, then the box below will have a link to your site or blog. It could also be a direct affiliate link for income, as at this time there are no restrictions on using affiliate links in Google+ posts.

http://Your Page, Blog, or Affiliate Link Goes Here   Add

Public ×   + Add more people

Share

searching on key phrases in your niche.

The image above is a post that's about to be shared publicly. You can see that you can write up as much text as you want, and then place either a direct affiliate link or a link to a landing page at your website or blog.

The link for "Add more people" allows you to add specific Circles, and you can even take out the public share and share only with specific Circles. How might this be useful for profits? As you build out this business page and post great information there, you're going to be found on the Web and people will place your page in their Circles. You get notified, and then you can place them into your Circles. When they share something you wrote, you'll be able to go to their profile and see which post interested them, and they either "+1" the post or share it.

If your niche is broad, you see where their interests lie once they do that. . Using our camping example again, you may be marketing for RV dealers, tent manufacturers, camping equip- ment, and other sub-niches. Once you see where someone's interests lie, you can place them in a Circle created just for that sub-niche.

This is a simplified way to do the equivalent of targeted email marketing as a follow-up activity. You have built a circle of people who have shown an interest in RV equipment and acces- sories. Later, if you want to place a direct affiliate link to a high paying RV accessory, you can both make the post public and also share it specifically with that Circle.

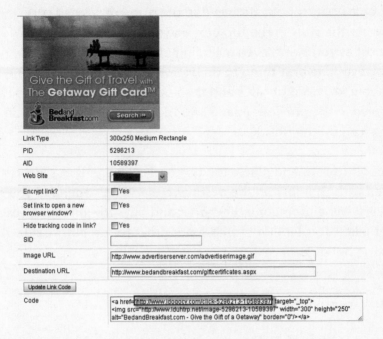

Posting Direct Affiliate Links Easily

The image above is a vendor affiliate merchant in the Commission Junction Network. I grab one of their commission links, copying out what you see in the box. Then I write a post on my

Google+ page about this vendor, the offer, or related stuff. I wrote the stuff in the top box, and you can write as long of a post as you want, even including affiliate links in the post. However, the best thing to do is to write a post that uses one of your keyword phrases and then paste the affiliate link as I copied in the previous image into the link add tool (the chain link icon on the right).

Google+ grabs and places the text and/or image that's associated with that link on the destination/landing page, and you're all set. When someone clicks on it and buys this gift card, you get paid. This type of promotion is great to run before gift-giving holidays.

Multiple Niche Pages

You can create as many pages as you want, and each can cover a different marketing niche. There are also features with the pages that allow you to place more permanent links down the right side of the page. These can be affiliate links to your major vendor sites that set a cookie, and the visitor can shop around on the site and you get paid if they buy while the cookie is in force.

The image above is of a Google+ business About page. The links on the right in this case are to searches within this page's posts to pull up specific topics by keywords. However, they could just as easily be direct affiliate links to specific information products, software, or hardware related to running a small business.

You can see from the image that you have tabs for your posts stream, the About page in the image, as well as for photos and videos. The posts stream page looks like this:

 You now have enough information to get started with affiliate marketing with Google+. It would be a good idea, and you should start reading about how Google+ is integrating the posts from there into regular Google searches for your niche keywords. And a major bonus is that anyone who has your page in their circles will see some of your posts high in their search results due to Google+'s new Personal Results function.

CHAPTER 17

Twitter as a Marketplace

As the image says, Twitter connects celebrities, friends, and experts. While you can't say a whole lot in a Tweet, you can make it a headline for what you want to sell and then create the short link directly to your affiliate commission page.

This is the most direct use of Twitter for affiliate marketers, but I'll show you some other ways to use Twitter to promote your own website and blog content on an automated basis. Whenever you write a blog post, a Google+ post, or content on a website, you can usually have some automated third party process create a Tweet for you to expand your exposure.

The image above shows the results of a search at http://search. twitter.com for "camping recipes." Notice the second result for the *Leave No Crumbs Camping Cookbook*. I don't know if the link is an Amazon Affiliate Link, but it certainly could be. Here's where the link takes the person who clicks on it:

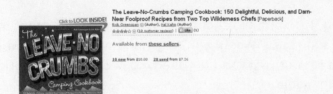

 So it's easy to just place direct affiliate links into Twitter with selling headline text and wait for the clicks. If you create a Twitter account for each niche, then you can promote all of your affiliate products and services through that niche account. As you build followers, you'll reach them directly with your marketing.

Feeding Other Content to Twitter
If you're blogging, there are plugins for WordPress and other

third party tools to automatically send a headline of your post content to Twitter with a link back to the original content. There are also tools out there to do it with Facebook posts, and extensions and third party tools to do the same with Google+ posts.

However, remember the Hootsuite tool I showed you back in the blogging chapter. It's the most efficient way for the affiliate marketer to connect multiple social media accounts together and automatically share content between them. Even if you need the Pro features, it's only $5.99/month. If you can't get that back many times over in commissions, you're probably not using it properly.

Twitter as a Headline & Connection Tool

While you can consider Twitter an affiliate commission-generating tool, there's another way to think of it that's valuable, as well. Think of using Twitter as a kind of Connection Tool. I'm not just talking about connecting people as social networks do, but connecting your marketing venues together.

By having Hootsuite or other tools cross-post your content from multiple sources as Tweets, you're generating back links, which are good for both SEO and for directing people to your various marketing media.

Remember I said you would have a slower process building Circles with Google+ pages due to the restrictions on adding people and commenting? However, if you set up your page posts to automatically go to a Twitter account in the niche, you will be building followers there in all of the ways Twitter allows. They'll see your Google+ page headlines, click over, and they'll add your page to their Circles.

You can even send them a simple invite with a Tweet like:
"Great information, cooking recipes, and camping news at Everything Camping at Google+ http://shortlinkhere"

CHAPTER 18

Commissions from Home – Go For It!

Let's just do some review in this last chapter to help you jump-start your affiliate commissions from your home business. There is a whole lot of information in this book, and it can be daunting if you're just starting out. However, it doesn't need to be, as you can quickly get started and build out your business at whatever pace you desire.

You can take your time because you don't have to spend any money to do most of what I've told you about here. So there's no pressure on you to get a certain amount of income flowing in order to pay your overhead ... there's no overhead!

Products & Services
You learned how money is made with affiliate commissions paid when your links bring a customer to a vendor/advertiser. We learned that there is affiliate income to be made from just about any product or service you can dream up.

Throughout the book, we found that we can market within a niche, like fitness, losing weight, camping, etc. In that niche, we found that there can be sub-niche markets, and that we can advertise hundreds of products and services in every niche we choose.

Information Products
I showed you how information products pay some of the highest commission percentages out there, many as high as 75% of the selling price. I showed you Clickbank and other information

product specialty networks and how they work to make money promoting reports, eBooks, DVDs, etc.

Affiliate Networks

No matter what type of product or service you are interested in, there will be companies you can find to represent. I showed you how to find affiliate signup links on company sites in order to set up an account. However, far more efficient is the affiliate network. I used Commission Junction as an example of a network representing hundreds of advertisers using tens of thousands of affiliates.

The network handles all of the details of connecting advertisers with publishers; that's us. Setting up an account with a network like Commission Junction, you can quickly connect with a great many advertisers for your marketing and link placement.

Automated Links with Skimlinks

For those who may already have sites or blogs up about niche topics, or for those who will be writing a lot of content, Skimlinks uses text in the content to automatically create affiliate links to advertisers in their network.

You can combine Skimlinks with other networks and individual affiliate accounts so you can take advantage of these automated links without extra effort in your writing. It's just one more way to make money from activities you're already doing in your marketing.

Websites & Blogs for Marketing

You learned about hosting accounts and setting up websites or blogging to create a lot of content related to your niche. This content will bring traffic to your site, and you place affiliate links in the content to generate income.

You learned that WordPress will let you set up a website and blog combined, and you can do it at no cost. I showed you that for a very small cost, you can host the blog yourself and take advantage of themes and plugins designed specifically for affiliate marketers.

We discovered methods of cross-posting, especially Hootsuite. This tool makes it easy to connect our various marketing venues and write something one time but use it in several places automatically.

SEO & SEM
Search Engine Optimization for the everyday Web content creator was explained. You learned some simple strategies to employ in all of your content to make it more search-engine-friendly and get better free position in search engine results for your best keywords and key phrases.

SEM, Search Engine Marketing, is paying for placement in the search engine results. I showed you how to set up an AdWords account and an ad campaign and keywords. You learned that you could completely control your budget, as well.

I gave you some really valuable information that many AdWords marketers don't realize. You now know that doing everything right in the creation of your ad title and text, as well as in your landing page content, will increase your CTR (Click-Through-Ratio), and Google rewards you by moving you up higher in the results but charging you less per click.

Commenting, Forums, Email and Article Marketing
In this chapter you learned how to go out and participate in discussion forums about your niche, as well as how to comment on blog posts in blogs about your market niche. These comments and discussion forum posts allow you to link back to your web-

site or blogs, as well as to place direct affiliate links if you want. You learned about writing articles for article sites in order to present yourself as an expert in your marketing niche, as well as to allow you to link back to your websites or blogs. This back linking improves your position in the search engines for your best niche keywords and phrases.

I showed you how to use forms on your sites to gather email addresses. Then you learned how to create drip email campaigns to build repeat income by following up with these email lists with informative emails containing your affiliate links.

Marketing on Facebook, Google+ & Twitter

There is a ton of information in those three chapters. Social media are consuming huge amounts of consumer time, and you can generate a lot of income just by properly using the social media to cross-promote and place affiliate links.

You learned how to connect your various social media accounts for cross-posting and directing your prospects from one place to another for profits. You learned how to use Facebook Fan Pages and Google+ Business Pages as business locations for each of your niche markets.

IS FOR QUARRY

SUE GRAFTON

a marian wood book

Published by G. P. Putnam's Sons
a member of
Penguin Putnam Inc.
New York